FRACTAL MYSTICISM: SACRED PATTERNS IN THE UNIVERSE

Chaos and Order: Understanding the Geometry of Magic

D.R. T STEPHENS

S.D.N Publishing

Copyright © 2023 S.D.N Publishing

All rights reserved

The characters and events portrayed in this book are fictitious. Any similarity to real persons, living or dead, is coincidental and not intended by the author.

No part of this book may be reproduced, or stored in a retrieval system, or transmitted in any form or by any means, electronic, mechanical, photocopying, recording, or otherwise, without express written permission of the publisher.

ISBN: 9798866331307

CONTENTS

Title Page
Copyright
General Disclaimer   1
Chapter 1: Welcoming the Enigma   3
Chapter 2: Fractals 101: An Introduction   6
Chapter 3: The Sacred Geometry Primer   10
Chapter 4: Understanding Chaos Theory   13
Chapter 5: Mathematical Mysticism   16
Chapter 6: Spirituality and Dimensions   19
Chapter 7: Recursion and the Infinite   22
Chapter 8: Natural Fractals: Trees, Rivers, and Clouds   25
Chapter 9: Early Historical Context of Mystical Geometry   28
Chapter 10: Alchemy and Fractal Patterns   31
Chapter 11: Esoteric Concepts of Space   34
Chapter 12: The Seed of Life   37
Chapter 13: Transformation and Symmetry   40
Chapter 14: Spirals in Mysticism   43
Chapter 15: Mandalas: Where Geometry and Spirituality Converge   45
Chapter 16: Quantum Connections   48
Chapter 17: The Complexity of Simplicity   52

Chapter 18: The Lore of Large Numbers	55
Chapter 19: The Golden Ratio and the Fibonacci Sequence	58
Chapter 20: Non-Euclidean Spaces	62
Chapter 21: The Hidden Dimensions	65
Chapter 22: Time, Fractals, and Eternity	68
Chapter 23: The Mystical Universe as a Hologram	71
Chapter 24: Cellular Automata and Spiritual Models	74
Chapter 25: Vibrational Frequency and Resonance	78
Chapter 26: The Mandelbrot Set and the Geometry of the Divine	81
Chapter 27: Paradoxes and Self-Reference	84
Chapter 28: Randomness and Determinism	87
Chapter 29: Crystallography and Spiritual Lattices	90
Chapter 30: The Zeno Phenomenon and Infinite Reduction	93
Chapter 31: Intersection of Fractals and Artificial Intelligence	96
Chapter 32: Psychoactive Substances and Altered States	99
Chapter 33: Cosmological Patterns and Cosmic Mysticism	102
Chapter 34: Quantum Computing and Mystical Complexity	105
Chapter 35: The Ethics of Mystical Geometry	109
Chapter 36: Multiverse Theories and Eternal Return	112
Chapter 37: The Uncertainty Principle and Divine Mystery	115
Chapter 38: The Fourth Dimension and Spiritual Ascension	118
Chapter 39: Gödel's Incompleteness Theorems and Spiritual Limitations	122
Chapter 40: Neural Networks and the Mind's Fractals	126

Chapter 41: Virtual Reality and Simulated Spirituality	129
Chapter 42: Fractal Economics and Spiritual Wealth	132
Chapter 43: Cybernetics and the Feedback Loop of Spirituality	136
Chapter 44: Chaos Magick and Contemporary Practices	140
Chapter 45: Exotic Matter and Anti-Matter: Beyond Physical Reality	143
Chapter 46: Transcending Language: Symbols, Sigils, and Scripts	146
Chapter 47: Confronting the Abyss: The Ultimate Fractal	149
Chapter 48: Concluding Reflections: The Beauty of Complexity	153
THE END	157

GENERAL DISCLAIMER

This book is intended to provide informative and educational material on the subject matter covered. The author(s), publisher, and any affiliated parties make no representations or warranties with respect to the accuracy, applicability, completeness, or suitability of the contents herein and specifically disclaim any implied warranties of merchantability or fitness for a particular purpose.

The information contained in this book is for general information purposes only and is not intended to serve as legal, medical, financial, or any other form of professional advice. Readers should consult with appropriate professionals before making any decisions based on the information provided. Neither the author(s) nor the publisher shall be held responsible or liable for any loss, damage, injury, claim, or otherwise, whether direct or indirect, consequential, or incidental, that may occur as a result of applying or misinterpreting the information in this book.

This book may contain references to third-party websites, products, or services. Such references do not constitute an endorsement or recommendation, and the author(s) and publisher are not responsible for any outcomes related to these third-party references.

In no event shall the author(s), publisher, or any affiliated parties be liable for any direct, indirect, punitive, special, incidental, or other consequential damages arising directly or indirectly from any use of this material, which is provided "as is," and without warranties of any kind, express or implied.

By reading this book, you acknowledge and agree that you assume all risks and responsibilities concerning the applicability and consequences of the information provided. You also agree to indemnify, defend, and hold harmless the author(s), publisher, and any affiliated parties from any and all liabilities, claims, demands, actions, and causes of action whatsoever, whether or not foreseeable, that may arise from using or misusing the information contained in this book.

Although every effort has been made to ensure the accuracy of the information in this book as of the date of publication, the landscape of the subject matter covered is continuously evolving. Therefore, the author(s) and publisher expressly disclaim responsibility for any errors or omissions and reserve the right to update, alter, or revise the content without prior notice.

By continuing to read this book, you agree to be bound by the terms and conditions stated in this disclaimer. If you do not agree with these terms, it is your responsibility to discontinue use of this book immediately.

CHAPTER 1: WELCOMING THE ENIGMA

In the labyrinthine corridors of the cosmos, where stars are born and galaxies spiral in a cosmic dance, there lies a hidden order, an enigmatic pattern that resonates through the fabric of reality. This order, complex yet undeniably symmetrical, whispers the ancient language of fractals, echoing the sacred geometry that has fascinated mystics, scientists, and philosophers alike. Welcome to "Fractal Mysticism: Sacred Patterns in the Universe," where we embark on an odyssey to decipher these cryptic messages, to understand the geometry of magic, and to fathom the profound interconnection between chaos and order.

The Language of the Universe

The universe speaks in the language of mathematics, a dialect woven from the threads of numbers, shapes, and patterns. Fractals, the heroes of our story, are the intricate patterns that repeat themselves on multiple scales, a phenomenon often referred to as self-similarity. From the branching of trees and the structure of snowflakes to the contours of coastlines and the spiral arms of galaxies, fractals are the fingerprints of nature's artistry.

But fractals are more than just mathematical curiosities; they are the brushstrokes of a greater canvas, a mystical tapestry that interweaves the physical with the metaphysical. This book is an invitation to explore the esoteric realm where fractals and mysticism converge, to peel back the layers of reality and glimpse the sacred patterns that lie beneath.

Geometry and Magic: An Unlikely Pair

At first glance, geometry and magic might seem like strange bedfellows—one grounded in the rigorous logic of mathematics and the other in the ethereal realms of the mystical. Yet, upon closer inspection, we find that they are two sides of the same coin. Sacred geometry, a term that evokes the reverence of ancient architects and the awe of modern-day seekers, is the study of the geometric patterns that are believed to be the fundamental building blocks of the universe. These patterns are not merely physical constructs; they are imbued with spiritual significance, embodying the principles of harmony, balance, and beauty that transcend the material world.

Magic, in its most profound sense, is the art of tapping into the unseen forces that govern the cosmos, of aligning oneself with the natural rhythms of creation. It is a dance with the divine geometry, a symphony played in the key of the universe. In this book, we explore the enchanting intersection of these two realms, where the logical meets the mystical, and the mundane meets the magical.

Embarking on a Mystical Journey

As we set out on this journey through "Fractal Mysticism," we will begin with the basics, gently unraveling the complexities of fractals and sacred geometry. In the early chapters, we will lay the foundations, exploring the simple yet profound principles that govern these patterns. We will delve into the historical and cultural significance of geometry in mystical traditions, uncovering the threads that weave through ancient and modern spiritual practices.

As our understanding deepens, we will venture into the intermediate realms, exploring the more intricate aspects of fractal mysticism. We will grapple with paradoxes, unravel the enigma of infinity, and ponder the philosophical implications of these sacred patterns. Our voyage will take us to the frontiers of science and spirituality, where we will encounter quantum mysteries and holographic universes.

Finally, in the advanced chapters, we will ascend to the zenith of complexity, confronting the grand questions that have perplexed humanity since time immemorial. We will explore the ethical dimensions of mystical geometry, the potential of quantum computing to model spiritual systems, and the philosophical conundrums that arise at the intersection of science and mysticism.

Our journey will conclude with a reflection on the beauty and awe that emerge from studying the intricate connections between fractals, mysticism, and the universe. We will emerge from this odyssey not only with a deeper understanding of the patterns that underlie reality but also with a renewed sense of wonder for the enigmatic tapestry of existence.

So, dear reader, let us step into the realm of fractal mysticism with open minds and hearts. Let us embrace the enigma, celebrate the mystery, and bask in the awe-inspiring beauty of the sacred patterns that dance through the universe. Welcome to a world where chaos and order, geometry and magic, coalesce in a symphony of cosmic proportions. Welcome to "Fractal Mysticism: Sacred Patterns in the Universe."

CHAPTER 2: FRACTALS 101: AN INTRODUCTION

Welcome to the fascinating world of fractals—a term that might sound intricate and abstruse at first glance, but which encapsulates an enormous realm of natural patterns, mathematical constructs, and even mystical insights. In this chapter, we'll gently unravel the complex tapestry of fractals, presenting their fundamental principles in a manner that's approachable yet comprehensive.

Understanding Fractals: A Conceptual Overview

Fractals are, in essence, never-ending patterns. They are characterized by their self-similarity, which means that the overall structure can be seen replicated in its smaller components. This intriguing property is not confined to mathematical concepts alone; fractals can be observed throughout the natural world, from the branching of trees to the formation of coastlines. It is as if nature has a penchant for this particular design scheme, utilizing it across different scales and contexts.

Mathematically, fractals are born out of a recursive process—a method of defining an operation in terms of itself. This recursive quality allows for an iterative building of the fractal's complexity. Each step in the process involves the repetition of a specific pattern or formula, and this repeated application leads to the fractal's intricately detailed architecture. The beauty of fractals lies in their infinite complexity; no matter how much one zooms in, there is always another layer of detail to explore.

Key Terms in Fractal Geometry

To fully appreciate fractals, it is essential to familiarize oneself with a few pivotal terms and concepts:

1. **Iteration**: This refers to the repetitive process of applying a particular set of rules or a mathematical formula over and over again.
2. **Self-similarity**: The property of a shape or pattern to look the same at different scales. In fractals, this often manifests as smaller copies of the whole being found within its parts.
3. **Dimensionality**: Fractals exhibit what is known as 'non-integer dimensions' or 'fractal dimensions.' This is a measure of their complexity and indicates that fractals can exist in between the traditional dimensions that we are familiar with.
4. **Mandelbrot Set**: Named after Benoît Mandelbrot, who is often referred to as the father of fractal geometry, the Mandelbrot Set is a particular set of complex numbers that forms a fractal when plotted on a complex plane.
5. **Julia Set**: Like the Mandelbrot Set, the Julia Set is a collection of points on a complex plane that exhibits fractal properties, resulting in intricate and beautiful patterns.

Fractals in Nature

The realm of fractals is not confined to mathematical textbooks. They are vividly present in the world around us. The branching pattern of trees, the spiral arrangement of a galaxy, the jagged coastline, and even the structure of snowflakes—all these are examples of natural fractals. They represent an underlying order in what might initially seem chaotic, an organized complexity that is both functional and aesthetically fascinating.

In recognizing these patterns, one begins to appreciate the harmony that exists between the realms of mathematics, nature, and even spirituality. Fractals, by their very nature, embody the idea of interconnectedness, demonstrating that similar principles can manifest in vastly different contexts, scales, and forms.

Fractals in Technology and Art

Fractals have found their applications in various technological fields. In digital imaging, fractal compression uses the self-similarity principle of fractals to store image data efficiently. In telecommunications, fractal antennas, with their intricate shapes, are used to capture signals due to their wide bandwidth and compact size. Moreover, the concepts of fractals have inspired numerous artists and architects who incorporate their complex, repetitive patterns into their creations, bridging the gap between science and art.

This chapter has provided a foundational understanding of fractals, painting a picture of their omnipresence and multifaceted nature. From the macrocosm of celestial bodies to the microcosm of our own biology, fractals emerge as a recurring theme, signifying a deeper order and symmetry in the universe. As we continue our exploration in subsequent chapters, we will delve into the sacred geometry that underpins spiritual practices, offering a more profound appreciation of the geometric tapestry that weaves together the fabric of existence.

CHAPTER 3: THE SACRED GEOMETRY PRIMER

Geometry, with its crisp lines and precise angles, might seem a world apart from the fluid realms of spirituality and mysticism. Yet, across cultures and epochs, sacred geometry has been revered as a conduit to the divine, offering a structural framework that underpins the very fabric of our universe. This chapter delves into the mystical significance of geometric shapes and patterns, revealing how they form a silent language that speaks of the cosmos, consciousness, and the interconnectedness of all things.

Sacred Shapes and their Spiritual Significance

At the heart of sacred geometry are foundational shapes and patterns revered in various spiritual traditions for their symbolic potency. The circle, embodying notions of eternity and unity due to its lack of a beginning or end, is prevalent in spiritual iconography. It often represents the divine, the soul, or the universe itself. Similarly, the square, with its four equal sides, is frequently associated with stability, materiality, and the earthly realm. Its orientation aligns with the cardinal directions, tying it to concepts of space and time.

The triangle, a shape found in pyramids and trines, holds

profound spiritual meaning as well. Its three sides have been linked to trinities found in different belief systems—such as the Father, Son, and Holy Spirit in Christianity, or the triad of Brahma, Vishnu, and Shiva in Hinduism. The upward-pointing triangle is often seen as a symbol of aspiration, rising energy, or masculine principle, while the downward-pointing triangle represents receptivity, surrender, or the feminine principle.

Interlocking Patterns and the Web of Life

As we move beyond simple shapes, sacred geometry reveals complex patterns that echo the interconnectedness of all things. The Flower of Life, a pattern composed of multiple evenly-spaced, overlapping circles, is one such example. This pattern, which can be extended infinitely, has been found in ancient temples, manuscripts, and artworks worldwide. It is said to represent the cycle of creation, encapsulating the fundamental forms of space and time. In this perfect geometric pattern, mystics and seekers have found a metaphor for the interconnectedness of life and spirit.

The Vesica Piscis, formed by the intersection of two circles with the same radius, is another sacred pattern. Its almond shape is a symbol of the divine feminine, the womb, and the gateway to life. It is the space of creation, where two distinct entities meet and give rise to new life. In the Christian tradition, the Vesica Piscis has been used to frame Christ in sacred art, symbolizing the intersection of the divine and the earthly.

Geometry in Spiritual Practices

Sacred geometry is not only a passive symbol but also an active element in various spiritual practices. In the construction of religious structures, such as churches, temples, mosques, and altars, sacred geometry provides not just aesthetic harmony but is believed to resonate with spiritual energies. For instance, the Gothic cathedrals of Europe are replete with geometric patterns that are thought to elevate the soul, drawing the mind towards the heavens through their towering spires and heavenly light filtered through stained glass windows.

Labyrinths, with their winding paths leading to a center, serve as another example. Often based on intricate geometric designs, they are used as a tool for meditation and spiritual journeying. The act of walking a labyrinth is symbolic of the pilgrimage towards one's own center, a path of introspection and contemplation.

Conclusion

In this exploration of sacred geometry, we have uncovered a dimension where mathematics and mysticism coalesce, where shapes and patterns are more than mere designs—they are imbued with profound spiritual significance. As we continue our journey through the realms of fractal mysticism, let us carry with us the understanding that the universe speaks in the language of geometry, a language that resonates with the core of our being and the cosmos beyond.

CHAPTER 4: UNDERSTANDING CHAOS THEORY

In the intricate dance of the universe, chaos and order seem to be eternal partners, waltzing in and out of each other's embrace. As we delve deeper into the realm of fractal mysticism, it's crucial to grasp the foundational concept of chaos theory and its intimate relationship with fractals. In this chapter, we'll explore the origins, key principles, and relevance of chaos theory to the mesmerizing patterns of fractals and its implications for spiritual and mystical perspectives.

1. The Origins of Chaos Theory

Chaos theory, despite its seemingly modern roots, has ancient philosophical undertones. Ancient cultures often grappled with the ideas of order and disorder, attempting to understand the unpredictable nature of the world around them. Fast forward to the 20th century, and the field began to gain traction as mathematicians and physicists started noticing unpredictable behaviors in deterministic systems, a phenomenon that defied traditional Newtonian physics.

The butterfly effect, one of the most iconic aspects of chaos theory, was popularized by meteorologist Edward Lorenz in the 1960s. He observed that minuscule changes in the initial conditions of a system could lead to vastly different outcomes. This notion, metaphorically explained, suggests that the flap of a butterfly's wings in Brazil could set off a tornado in Texas. The butterfly effect illustrates the sensitivity of chaotic systems and the intricate interplay of elements within them.

2. Core Principles of Chaos Theory

Determinism and Predictability: At the heart of chaos theory lies a profound paradox: deterministic yet unpredictable. Systems governed by chaos theory follow deterministic laws, meaning they are not random. However, due to their sensitivity to initial conditions, predicting long-term behaviors becomes virtually impossible. This delicate balance challenges our understanding of determinism, pushing us to reconsider the nature of predictability in the universe.

Fractals and Strange Attractors: As chaotic systems evolve, they often exhibit fractal patterns, also known as strange attractors. These attractors, while having a non-repeating pattern, have a structure that is self-similar across different scales. This self-similarity, or recursion, is a hallmark of fractals and forms the bridge between chaos theory and fractal mysticism. The Mandelbrot Set, for instance, is a visual representation of such a chaotic system, where each iteration reveals deeper layers of complexity.

Order within Chaos: One of the most profound insights of chaos theory is the discovery of order within apparent disorder. When observed from a distance, chaotic systems may seem random and devoid of any pattern. Yet, a closer look often unveils intricate structures and repeating motifs. This inherent order within chaos resonates deeply with spiritual and mystical teachings, suggesting that even in the midst of life's unpredictabilities, there exists an underlying cosmic order.

3. Chaos Theory and Spiritual Implications

The intertwining of chaos theory and spirituality offers rich insights into the nature of existence. Just as chaos theory challenges our understanding of predictability, spiritual teachings often encourage us to embrace uncertainty, urging us to find meaning in life's unpredictable twists and turns.

Moreover, the inherent order found within chaos mirrors spiritual beliefs of a cosmic order or divine plan governing the universe. This perspective fosters a deeper understanding and acceptance of life's unpredictabilities, framing them not as random occurrences, but as intricate parts of a grander design.

Furthermore, the self-similar patterns of fractals found in chaotic systems echo the hermetic axiom "As above, so below," suggesting that patterns observed in the macrocosm are reflected in the microcosm and vice versa. This interconnectedness and reflection of patterns across scales resonate deeply with many spiritual traditions, emphasizing unity and the interconnected nature of all existence.

In summary, chaos theory, with its delicate balance of determinism and unpredictability, offers a fresh lens through which we can explore and appreciate the intricacies of the universe. Its intimate relationship with fractals deepens our understanding of sacred patterns, intertwining science and spirituality in a harmonious dance. As we continue our journey into fractal mysticism, the insights from chaos theory serve as a beacon, illuminating the paths of both the scientist and the mystic.

CHAPTER 5: MATHEMATICAL MYSTICISM

Mathematics, the universal language of the cosmos, has whispered secrets to those attuned to its nuances throughout history. Its symbiotic relationship with mysticism is profound, tethered through numbers and formulas that transcend mere calculation to touch the very essence of existence. This chapter delves into the profound and sometimes enigmatic ways in which mathematics has been employed in mystical practices, unveiling how numbers and equations have not merely been tools for constructing realities but also for interpreting the cosmos's enigmatic language.

Numbers: The Cosmic Code

Since ancient times, numbers have held a sacred significance, believed to be the foundational elements of the universe. From Pythagoras, who averred that numbers constitute the true nature of things, to the Kabbalists, who sought divine wisdom in the numerical interpretation of the Hebrew scriptures, numbers have been more than mere symbols; they are the metaphysical threads weaving the tapestry of existence.

Numerology, the mystical study of numbers, posits that each number possesses its own vibrational frequency and divine significance. The number one, for instance, symbolizes unity and the origin of all things, while the number two represents duality, balance, and the relational nature of existence. This esoteric discipline reveals an interconnected universe, where numbers are not just for arithmetic but also keys to understanding the mystical laws governing reality.

Sacred Formulas: Geometry of the Gods

Just as individual numbers hold sacred connotations, mathematical formulas and constants are revered for their mystical properties. The golden ratio, an irrational number approximately equal to 1.618, appears ubiquitously in nature, art, and architecture. This proportion, epitomizing beauty and harmony, has been hailed as a divine blueprint, an archetype imprinted in the cosmos, echoing the ancient Hermetic principle "As above, so below."

Mathematical patterns and formulas are revered not merely for their aesthetic allure but also for their ontological implications. The Fibonacci sequence, a series of numbers where each is the sum of the two preceding ones, manifests in the spirals of galaxies and the growth patterns of plants. Such recursive patterns are seen as fractal expressions of the divine mind, a cosmic algorithm iterating across the vast canvas of reality.

Transcendental Numbers: Portals to Infinity

Transcendental numbers, such as pi (π) and e (Euler's number), hold a special place in the pantheon of mathematical mysticism. These numbers, irrational and non-algebraic, cannot be derived from any finite sequence of algebraic operations. Pi, the ratio of a circle's circumference to its diameter, is not only ubiquitous in geometric calculations but also symbolizes the ineffable mystery of the cosmos, an endless decimal mirroring the universe's boundless nature.

Euler's number, e, fundamental to the field of calculus, governs growth and decay processes, from radioactive decay to population dynamics. Mystics have long marveled at how such constants underpin the fabric of reality, hinting at a deeper, unseen order. In transcendental numbers, we find the fingerprints of the ineffable, the mathematical echoes of the infinite.

Conclusion: The Language of the Divine

As we've journeyed through the mathematical landscapes that pervade mysticism, we uncover a universe inscribed with the language of numbers. Mathematical mysticism does not reduce the sacred to equations; rather, it reveals the inherent sacredness in the mathematical order of the cosmos. It's a realm where numbers are not just quantities but qualities, each imbued with esoteric significance. Here, mathematics is not the cold, sterile realm of the calculative mind but a vibrant tapestry woven with the threads of the divine.

This chapter serves as a testament to the profundity of numbers and formulas in mystical traditions. The journey of understanding how mathematical mysticism shapes our interpretation of the universe is one that requires both rational and intuitive faculties, for the cosmos whispers its secrets not just in the language of logic but also in the silence between numbers, in the gaps where infinity dwells.

CHAPTER 6: SPIRITUALITY AND DIMENSIONS

In the quest for spiritual understanding, the concept of dimensions occupies a crucial juncture, providing a bridge between the tangible and the metaphysical. This chapter delves into the enigmatic relationship between spirituality and dimensions, exploring how higher dimensions have found resonance within various spiritual traditions and how they shape our understanding of the cosmos.

Interdimensional Mysticism

The notion of dimensions extends beyond the three spatial dimensions and time that we experience in our daily lives. Mystics and spiritual seekers often speak of higher dimensions as realms of consciousness that transcend our ordinary perceptions. These dimensions are not just additional spaces but are intricately connected to states of being, levels of awareness, and layers of reality. In many spiritual traditions, the ascent through higher dimensions is synonymous with spiritual evolution, a journey that takes one closer to the divine or ultimate reality.

In the context of fractal mysticism, dimensions play a vital role. Fractals can be seen as the geometric representation of this interdimensional journey. They offer a glimpse into the complexity and interconnectedness of these higher realms. For instance, the Mandelbrot set, a famous fractal, exhibits an infinite depth of detail that hints at the boundless nature of higher dimensions. It serves as a metaphor for the spiritual path, where each step reveals deeper layers of understanding and connection.

Spiritual Dimensions and Quantum Physics

Quantum physics has introduced a profound shift in our understanding of dimensions. Theories like string theory suggest the existence of multiple spatial dimensions beyond our perceptible three. These theoretical frameworks resonate with mystical beliefs about higher dimensions. Just as quantum physics posits that particles can exist in multiple states simultaneously, spiritual traditions suggest that higher dimensions encompass a realm where ordinary rules of time and space do not apply, and multiple realities can coexist.

The parallels between quantum dimensions and spiritual dimensions open intriguing possibilities. Could these additional quantum dimensions be the same as the spiritual realms spoken of in mystical texts? This convergence of science and spirituality offers a fertile ground for exploration, suggesting that the universe is far more complex and interconnected than our senses reveal.

The Dimension of Consciousness

Consciousness itself can be viewed as a dimension—one that transcends physical space. In many spiritual teachings, consciousness is the fabric of the universe, an omnipresent dimension that connects all of existence. This perspective aligns with the concept of non-locality in quantum mechanics, where particles can influence each other instantaneously, regardless of the distance separating them.

In fractal mysticism, consciousness is the underlying pattern that weaves through the tapestry of the universe, much like the recurring patterns in fractals. It is both immanent and transcendent, present in the smallest particle and spanning the vastness of the cosmos. By aligning with this dimension of consciousness, practitioners of fractal mysticism aim to tap into the universal patterns that govern the dance of creation.

Conclusion

The exploration of spirituality and dimensions opens a window into the profound interconnectedness of all things. Dimensions are not just spatial constructs but are deeply woven into the fabric of our spiritual understanding. They offer a framework for contemplating the vastness of the universe and our place within it. As we continue our journey through "Fractal Mysticism: Sacred Patterns in the Universe," we carry with us the awareness of these higher dimensions and the infinite possibilities they hold for spiritual growth and cosmic insight.

CHAPTER 7: RECURSION AND THE INFINITE

Recursion is a phenomenon that lies at the heart of fractals, mysticism, and our understanding of the infinite. This chapter delves into the concept of recursion, exploring its role in the creation of fractal patterns and its profound implications in mystical traditions. It's a journey into the depths of the self-similar and the endless, where patterns repeat ad infinitum, each iteration a microcosm of the whole.

The Essence of Recursion

Recursion occurs when a process, whether it's a mathematical function, a natural pattern, or a spiritual practice, repeats itself within its own output. In mathematics, a recursive function is one that calls upon itself to solve a problem, creating an ongoing loop. This same principle manifests in the natural world in the form of fractals. For instance, consider the Romanesco broccoli, whose spiraled cones are composed of smaller, similarly spiraled cones. Each of these, in turn, is made of even smaller spiraled cones, continuing this pattern potentially to the cellular level.

In mystical traditions, recursion is often symbolized by the ouroboros, the ancient symbol of a serpent eating its own tail. This represents the eternal cycle of renewal and the infinite nature of the universe. Just as the serpent consumes itself only to be reborn from itself, recursion suggests that within every part of the universe, no matter how minute, lies the imprint of the whole.

Recursive Patterns in Mystical Traditions

Many mystical traditions have revered recursive patterns, viewing them as representations of the divine or the infinite. The recursive nature of mandalas, for instance, is thought to symbolize the universe and its endless cycles of birth, death, and rebirth. Each section of a mandala contains elements of the whole, creating a visual recursion that reflects the interconnectedness of all things.

Similarly, the concept of recursion is evident in the spiritual practice of chanting or meditation. A mantra, repeated over and over, is a form of recursive practice, where each repetition delves deeper into the consciousness. It's akin to a fractal pattern of thought, where each iteration takes the practitioner closer to enlightenment or a state of higher understanding, reflecting the infinite within the finite confines of the human experience.

The Infinite in the Finite

The beauty of recursion, especially in the context of fractals, lies in the infinite complexity that arises from simplicity. A simple recursive algorithm, when iterated countless times, can produce patterns of staggering complexity and beauty, such as the Mandelbrot set. This set, which will be explored in depth in later chapters, is a testament to the profound implications of recursion. It suggests that within the simple rules of the universe, there's the potential for infinite complexity and variation.

In mystical thought, this translates to the idea that within the simplicity of the divine, or the foundational truths of the universe, there's infinite depth and complexity. It implies that by understanding the recursive patterns of the cosmos, one can gain insights into the nature of existence and the divine. It's a concept that bridges science and spirituality, suggesting that the search for meaning, whether through mathematics or mysticism, is a recursive journey into the infinite.

Summary

Recursion is a foundational concept in both fractal geometry and mystical traditions. It represents the self-similar, the infinite in the finite, and the complex arising from the simple. As we've explored in this chapter, recursion manifests in the natural world, in mathematics, and in spiritual practices, each reflecting the infinite complexity of the universe. It's a concept that challenges our understanding of reality, suggesting that within every part of the cosmos, no matter how small, lies the essence of the whole, endlessly repeating into eternity.

CHAPTER 8: NATURAL FRACTALS: TREES, RIVERS, AND CLOUDS

Amidst the intricate dance of chaos and order, the geometry of nature unfurls in patterns that seem both random and yet profoundly intentional. These patterns, found in the branches of trees, the meandering paths of rivers, and the billowing formations of clouds, are more than mere coincidences; they are fractals, the language of the cosmos spoken through the dialect of the Earth. In this chapter, we delve into the mystical interpretations of these natural fractals, seeking to understand the silent wisdom they whisper to those who dare to listen.

The Arboreal Network: Trees and Fractals

Trees, in their silent stature, are amongst the most visually arresting examples of natural fractals. The way a tree branches, splitting from the main trunk into smaller and smaller limbs, mirrors a fractal process called self-similarity, where a pattern is repeated at different scales. But the mysticism of trees extends beyond their structure; it delves into the metaphysical.

In various mystical traditions, trees are seen as symbols of life, growth, and the connection between the heavens and the earth. The fractal nature of their branching can be seen as a reflection of the cosmic order, a tangible manifestation of the same patterns that govern the stars and galaxies. This parallel between the microcosm and macrocosm is a recurring theme in fractal mysticism, hinting at an underlying unity that transcends scale and form.

River Veins: The Meandering Paths of Water

Rivers, too, carve fractal patterns as they journey across landscapes. Their meandering paths, viewed from above, reveal a network of tributaries and streams that mirror the branching of trees and even the veins in our own bodies. This self-similar pattern, known as dendritic drainage, is not just a coincidence; it's a result of the natural processes of erosion and the flow of water seeking the path of least resistance.

In the mystical context, rivers have been seen as symbols of the flow of life and spiritual energy. Their fractal patterns can be interpreted as the flow of cosmic energy through the universe, branching and splitting, yet always part of a greater whole. The idea that the same patterns govern the veins of leaves, the branching of rivers, and even our own circulatory systems is a testament to the interconnectedness of all things, a core principle in many mystical beliefs.

Celestial Art: The Fractals of Clouds

Clouds, with their ever-changing forms, are another example of fractals in nature. The way clouds form, grow, and dissipate is governed by the principles of turbulence, a chaotic process that nonetheless gives rise to fractal structures. The edges of clouds, where they meet the clear sky, are often fractal boundaries, intricate and complex.

In mysticism, clouds have been seen as the abode of the divine, the place where the heavens touch the earth. Their fractal edges can be seen as the interface between the material and the spiritual, a threshold where order emerges from chaos. The transient nature of clouds, forming and re-forming in an endless cycle, speaks to the impermanence and constant flux that many mystical traditions emphasize.

Mystical Interpretations: A Deeper Understanding

These natural fractals are not just scientific curiosities; they are symbols, metaphors for the deeper workings of the universe. They remind us that the same patterns repeat at different scales, from the smallest leaf to the grandest galaxy. In recognizing these patterns, one can see the signatures of a deeper order, a cosmic geometry that underlies all of creation.

For the fractal mystic, these patterns are a source of spiritual insight. They teach us about the unity of all things, the interconnectedness of the cosmos, and the delicate balance between order and chaos. By observing and contemplating these natural fractals, one can gain a glimpse into the hidden workings of the universe, and perhaps, find a greater sense of harmony with the world around us.

In conclusion, the fractal patterns found in trees, rivers, and clouds are more than mere coincidences of nature; they are expressions of the sacred geometry that pervades the universe. They offer a visual and tangible connection to the mystical, a way to understand the ineffable patterns that bind all things in a cosmic dance of chaos and order. As we continue our journey through the realms of fractal mysticism, let these natural fractals be a reminder of the profound mysteries that await those who seek to unravel the sacred patterns of the universe.

CHAPTER 9: EARLY HISTORICAL CONTEXT OF MYSTICAL GEOMETRY

The quest for understanding the cosmos has perennially been intertwined with the enigmatic allure of geometry. This chapter embarks on a temporal voyage to explore how ancient civilizations perceived the mystical aspects of geometry, unearthing the rudimentary foundations that have shaped the modern conception of fractal mysticism.

Ancient Civilizations and Sacred Geometry

Geometry, derived from the Ancient Greek words 'geo' meaning 'earth', and 'metron' meaning 'measurement', was not merely a mathematical pursuit but a profound spiritual endeavor. Ancient civilizations, including the Egyptians, Greeks, and Indians, believed that geometric principles were inherent in the creation and structure of the cosmos. For them, sacred geometry was not just about the measurement of the earth, but about unraveling the cosmic blueprint.

The Egyptians, for example, were master geometers, as evident in the precision of their architectural marvels like the pyramids. They believed in the concept of 'Ma'at', which represented order, balance, and cosmic harmony. The meticulous geometry of their structures was a manifestation of 'Ma'at', aligning their terrestrial creations with celestial perfection.

In Ancient Greece, philosophers like Pythagoras and Plato were among the pioneers who delved into the mystical properties of geometry. Pythagoras is renowned for his theorem, but less known is his belief in the spiritual essence of numbers and shapes. He and his followers, the Pythagoreans, revered simple geometric forms like the triangle, considering them as the building blocks of reality, resonating with harmonious frequencies.

Plato, on the other hand, posited his theory of the 'Forms', abstract perfect entities, of which the physical world was just an imperfect reflection. His allegory of the cave illustrates this concept, with the shadows on the wall representing the physical world and the objects casting the shadows being the perfect Forms. The 'Platonic Solids', a set of polyhedra special for their symmetry, were considered by Plato to be the foundational geometries of the elemental constituents of the universe.

Mystical Aspects of Geometry in Vedic Traditions

In the ancient Vedic tradition of India, geometry was paramount in both architecture and spiritual symbolism. The 'Vastu Shastra', an ancient Indian system of architecture, incorporates geometric principles to harmonize structures with nature and cosmic energies. Another significant geometrical motif is the 'Sri Yantra', a complex geometrical figure used in meditation, representing the union of the divine masculine and feminine, encapsulating the concept of cosmic creation and harmony.

Geometry and the Celestial Harmony

Across these ancient civilizations, a recurrent theme is the profound belief in a cosmic order, a celestial harmony that governs the universe. This cosmic order was perceived to be geometric in nature, with shapes, proportions, and patterns believed to resonate with the frequencies of the cosmos. The celestial bodies, the cycles of seasons, and the growth patterns in nature—all were seen as manifestations of this cosmic geometry.

Geometry was a bridge between the earthly and the divine, a tool that allowed these civilizations to align their spiritual practices, architectural designs, and artistic expressions with the perceived order of the cosmos. The use of geometric patterns in temples, sacred texts, and ritualistic art was a means of connecting with the divine, of aligning oneself with the cosmic symphony.

In summary, the ancient historical context of mystical geometry reveals a world where mathematics and spirituality were not segregated but seamlessly intertwined. Geometry was not just about measurements and calculations but was imbued with a sacred essence, seen as the language of the cosmos itself. These early conceptualizations and practices laid the foundational stones for the modern exploration of fractal mysticism, serving as a testament to humanity's enduring quest to decipher the sacred patterns that weave the tapestry of the universe.

CHAPTER 10: ALCHEMY AND FRACTAL PATTERNS

Alchemy, often seen as a precursor to modern chemistry, was a discipline steeped in both scientific endeavor and mystical quest. At the heart of alchemy was the transformation, not only of base metals into noble ones but also of the alchemist's soul into a spiritually enlightened state. This chapter delves into the intricate relationship between alchemical symbols, which are rich in geometric forms, and the fractal geometry that we see threaded throughout the natural world and mystical experiences.

Alchemical Symbols and Geometry

Alchemical symbols are a language of their own, cryptic and full of layered meanings. The alchemists used these symbols not only to represent substances and processes but also to convey deeper spiritual truths. Many of these symbols are geometric in nature, such as the circle, square, and triangle, which often represent the spiritual trinity of body, soul, and spirit. These shapes are foundational to fractal geometry as well; they are the simple forms from which infinitely complex patterns can emerge through recursive processes.

The Ouroboros, an ancient symbol depicting a serpent eating its own tail, is another prime example of geometry in alchemical symbolism. It represents the cyclic nature of the universe—creation out of destruction, life out of death. This symbol is fractal in its essence: a loop that feeds back into itself, a boundary that is constantly being redrawn. It echoes the recursive process that is central to fractals, where the output of one iteration becomes the input for the next.

The Philosophers' Stone: A Fractal Process

Central to alchemical lore is the Philosophers' Stone, a legendary substance said to enable the transmutation of lead into gold and grant immortality. The process of creating the Philosophers' Stone, known as the Magnum Opus or Great Work, is deeply fractal in nature. It is not a linear process but a cyclical one involving stages of dissolution, purification, and reunification—each stage a transformation that is a reflection of the whole. The alchemists believed that by repeating these processes, both on a material and a spiritual level, one could arrive at a state of perfection. This mirrors the way fractals are generated, where a simple process repeated over and over can lead to incredibly complex and beautiful patterns.

Alchemy in the Natural World

Fractal patterns are abundant in nature: from the branching of trees to the structure of snowflakes, nature seems to favor fractal geometries. Alchemists, in their contemplation of nature, recognized this tendency and saw it as a reflection of the divine. In alchemical thought, the microcosm reflects the macrocosm; the patterns found in the natural world are also found within the human soul and the universe at large. This belief resonates with the modern understanding of fractals, where the same patterns can be seen at different scales, from the microscopic to the cosmic.

The Alchemical Mandala

The mandala, a geometric configuration of symbols, is a concept shared by many mystical traditions, including alchemy. In alchemical illustrations, mandalas often depict the union of opposites, the harmonization of the four elements, or the stages of the Magnum Opus. These mandalas are fractal in nature: they can be read at different levels, each level a microcosm of the whole. The center of the mandala, often represented by a circle or a rose, is akin to the seed of a fractal pattern, containing within it the blueprint for the entire structure.

Conclusion

Alchemy, with its rich symbolism and quest for transformation, provides a fascinating lens through which to explore fractal patterns. The geometric symbols used by alchemists reflect a deep understanding of the recursive and self-similar patterns found in nature and the human spirit. By examining the intersection of alchemy and fractal geometry, we gain insights into the ancient wisdom that saw the universe as an interconnected and infinitely unfolding mystery, a view that continues to resonate in the modern understanding of fractals and the sacred patterns that weave through the cosmos.

CHAPTER 11: ESOTERIC CONCEPTS OF SPACE

Space, in its most enigmatic forms, has long fascinated mystics, philosophers, and scientists alike. In the realm of the esoteric, space is not merely a physical dimension, but a vast canvas where the spiritual and the material intertwine in a dance of cosmic proportions. This chapter delves into the mystical traditions that view space not just as an empty expanse, but as a living, breathing entity imbued with sacred geometry and divine significance.

The Fabric of the Cosmos

In many esoteric teachings, space is regarded as a fabric, woven with the threads of existence itself. It's not an inert void but a dynamic, interactive field that responds to the vibrations of thought, emotion, and spiritual presence. This fabric is often visualized as a tapestry of intricate patterns, each thread representing a connection between points of consciousness. In such a view, to navigate space is to traverse a web of relationships, where every action, every intention, reverberates through the cosmic loom, altering the pattern of the whole.

This concept parallels with modern scientific theories, such as the fabric of spacetime in Einstein's General Relativity, where gravity is not a force exerted by masses, but a curvature in the fabric of spacetime caused by those masses. Similarly, in the esoteric view, spiritual entities and forces create curvatures and patterns in the fabric of cosmic space, influencing the flow of energy and the unfolding of events.

Dimensions Beyond Perception

Esoteric traditions often speak of dimensions beyond the familiar three-dimensional space. These are realms that exist parallel to our own, interpenetrating our reality and sometimes intersecting with it in ways that are inexplicable to the conventional mind. Such dimensions are not just extensions in a spatial sense but realms of higher consciousness, each with its own laws, entities, and possibilities.

Mystical practices aim to attune the practitioner to these higher dimensions, allowing glimpses into realms where space and time behave in ways alien to our normal perceptions. In some teachings, these dimensions are accessed through altered states of consciousness, meditation, or the use of sacred geometry, which serves as a bridge between the physical and the spiritual worlds.

The Living Space

In the esoteric view, space is alive. It is not a passive container for objects and events but an active participant in the cosmic play. This living space is imbued with intelligence and consciousness, responding to the intentions and actions of beings within it. Mystics and shamans have long held that space itself can be communicated with, appeased, or even commanded.

The concept of living space resonates with the idea of a universe that is fundamentally interconnected. Quantum entanglement, a phenomenon where particles remain connected regardless of the distance separating them, suggests that at a fundamental level, the universe is a unified whole. In the esoteric perspective, this wholeness extends beyond physical particles to the very fabric of space, which is alive with the dance of quantum fields and spiritual energies.

In conclusion, the esoteric concepts of space challenge our conventional understanding of reality. They invite us to view space not as a passive backdrop but as a dynamic, interconnected, and living tapestry of existence. By exploring these mystical perspectives, we broaden our perception of the cosmos and open ourselves to the profound mysteries that lie beyond the reach of the naked eye. In the grand tapestry of the universe, every thread, every pattern holds the potential for deep spiritual revelation.

CHAPTER 12: THE SEED OF LIFE

In the realm of fractal mysticism, geometric forms are not mere mathematical constructs but serve as conduits to the divine, bridging the physical and metaphysical realms. Among these sacred geometries, the "Seed of Life" occupies a revered place, for it is not only a symbol replete with profound meaning but also a foundational pattern, a matrix from which the fabric of existence is woven.

Unveiling the Seed of Life

At its core, the Seed of Life is a symbol consisting of seven circles. Six are symmetrically clustered around a central one, forming a design that resembles a flower or a seed, thus its name. This basic yet intricate pattern is the embryonic form of the Flower of Life, an even more complex symbol that has captivated human imagination for millennia.

The Seed of Life is thought to encapsulate the very essence of the universe. It is a geometric archetype found in various cultures and spiritual traditions, each attributing to it their own layers of meaning and interpretation. Some view it as a representation of the seven days of creation, a blueprint of the universe's genesis. Others see it as a symbol of the chakras, the energy centers in the body, or the seven classical planets in astrology.

Geometrical and Mystical Aspects

Geometrically, the Seed of Life is a marvel of symmetry and balance. It demonstrates how a simple repetitive process—drawing circles whose centers are on the circumference of the previous one—can give rise to an elegant and complex form. This recursive process is reminiscent of the principles of fractal geometry, where repeating a simple process can lead to infinitely complex patterns.

Mystically, the Seed of Life is more than a pattern; it is a form of visual meditation, a portal to the ineffable. Contemplating its interlocking circles, one can meditate on the interconnectedness of all life, the cyclical nature of existence, and the underlying unity behind apparent diversity. It serves as a reminder that every component of the universe, no matter how minute or seemingly inconsequential, is an integral part of the grand cosmic design.

The Seed and the Cosmos

The Seed of Life is not just a static symbol; it represents dynamic principles fundamental to our understanding of the cosmos. Just as the seed contains within it the potential for a whole plant, this symbol is believed to contain within its geometry the information for all of life. It's a concept that parallels the idea of the holographic universe, where every part contains information about the whole.

Furthermore, in fractal geometry, simple patterns can generate complex structures. The Seed of Life, with its recursive circle-drawing process, can be extended to form the Flower of Life, and from there, the Fruit of Life, which some believe contains the blueprint for the entire universe, including the Platonic solids—the building blocks of matter according to Greek philosophy.

The chapter explores the Seed of Life as a cornerstone of sacred geometry and fractal mysticism. It elucidates the symbol's geometric and mystical aspects, its significance in various spiritual traditions, and its metaphorical representation of universal principles. Through this exploration, the chapter reveals the Seed of Life as more than just a symbol; it is a microcosmic reflection of the cosmos, a blueprint for existence itself.

CHAPTER 13: TRANSFORMATION AND SYMMETRY

In the mesmerizing realm of fractal mysticism, transformation and symmetry do not merely play a role; they constitute the very heart of sacred patterns. Symmetry, in its most profound essence, embodies balance—a harmonious dance of proportions and ratios that echoes through the natural world, spiritual symbolism, and the enigmatic fractals that we encounter both in meditative practices and the mathematical sphere.

The Essence of Symmetry in Fractals

Symmetry, in the fractal context, is more than a mirror reflection or a rotational invariant; it's an expression of a deeper, almost ineffable truth about the universe. Fractals, with their self-similar patterns, illustrate symmetry not just across spatial dimensions but through the scales of size and complexity. The iteration of a simple rule can give birth to an infinitely complex system, which, no matter how closely or distantly you observe, maintains its core structural integrity—a testament to the transformative power of symmetry.

Consider the famous fractal shapes like the Sierpinski Triangle or the Mandelbrot Set. At first glance, they might seem merely intriguing, but a closer inspection reveals that these shapes are teeming with symmetry. Each triangle within the Sierpinski formation is a smaller version of the whole, and every contour in the Mandelbrot Set reflects a similar pattern ad infinitum. This recursive symmetry isn't just a mathematical curiosity; it's a whisper from the universe about the nature of reality itself.

Spiritual Symbolism and Symmetry

The concept of symmetry transcends the boundaries of mathematics and finds profound resonance in spiritual symbolism. Symmetrical forms are revered in various spiritual traditions for their perceived connection to the divine. From the bilateral symmetry of the human form, often seen as a reflection of the image of God in various theologies, to the intricate symmetrical designs of Islamic art, which symbolize the unchanging nature of the divine, symmetry is an embodiment of perfection and balance.

Moreover, consider the yin and yang symbol from Taoism, an epitome of symmetry and balance. It encapsulates the harmony of opposites—light and dark, male and female, chaos and order—suggesting that the universe inherently strives for equilibrium. This balance is reflective of the fractal nature of reality, where chaos and order are not antagonists but co-creators of the intricate tapestry of existence.

Transformation Through Fractal Symmetry

The journey through fractal mysticism is one of transformation. The understanding that symmetry in fractals is not static but dynamic—constantly evolving yet maintaining its essence—has profound spiritual implications. It reflects the transformative journey of the soul, which, despite the vicissitudes of life, retains its intrinsic nature.

The fractal's capacity to morph and scale, to become complex or simplified without losing its symmetry, is a metaphor for the soul's resilience and adaptability. In meditation and spiritual practices, the contemplation of fractal symmetry can lead to profound insights into the nature of the self and the cosmos. It becomes a meditative process, a transformational journey that echoes the recursive symmetry of fractals, leading one deeper into the understanding of the self and the universe.

In conclusion, transformation and symmetry are not merely concepts but experiences woven deeply into the fabric of fractal mysticism. They reveal the inherent order in chaos, the balance in the cosmos, and the transformative journey of the soul. As we delve deeper into the symmetrical patterns of fractals, we uncover not just mathematical truths but spiritual revelations that resonate with the symmetrical harmony of the universe itself.

CHAPTER 14: SPIRALS IN MYSTICISM

The spiral, a curve that emanates from a point, moving farther away as it revolves around the point, is a pattern that can be found throughout the natural world and has also wound its way deeply into the fabric of mystical teachings. This chapter delves into the rich symbolism of spirals in various mystical traditions, their presence in natural fractal patterns, and the deeper meanings they may hold in the context of fractal mysticism.

The Archetypal Spiral

In many ancient cultures, the spiral was seen as a symbol of growth, expansion, and cosmic energy. It was often associated with the journey from the outer consciousness to the inner soul, or vice versa, representing a path of evolution or a journey towards enlightenment. The way a spiral can seem to go on infinitely, getting either infinitely smaller or infinitely larger, aligns with many mystical teachings about the nature of the universe and the soul's progression through various planes of existence.

Spirals in Nature and Fractals

Spirals are not just symbolic constructs; they are also found abundantly in nature, providing a tangible connection between the mystical and the material. For example, the Fibonacci spiral, a geometric pattern derived from the Fibonacci sequence, is famously manifested in the nautilus shell, hurricanes, and even galaxies. This specific spiral is a type of fractal, displaying self-similarity as it maintains its shape regardless of the scale at which you observe it. The recurrence of spirals in nature hints at an underlying order in the chaos of the universe, a concept central to fractal mysticism.

The Spiral Dance

In various mystical practices, the spiral is often incorporated into rituals and dances. These movements mimic the cosmic dance of the planets and the stars, believed to be guided by a divine geometric pattern. The spiral dance is thus seen as a way to align oneself with the rhythms of the cosmos, achieving a sense of unity with the greater whole. The dancers, moving in a pattern that mirrors the fractal spirals found in nature, seek to attune themselves to the sacred patterns that permeate existence.

In summary, spirals serve as a profound link between the seen and the unseen, the tangible and the intangible, the scientific and the mystical. They remind us that the patterns we observe in the physical world may have deeper, spiritual significance, and that the universe might be more interconnected than we realize. Through the study of spirals in fractal mysticism, we begin to see how the microcosm reflects the macrocosm, and how the journey of the soul can be understood through the lens of sacred geometry.

CHAPTER 15: MANDALAS: WHERE GEOMETRY AND SPIRITUALITY CONVERGE

Within the vibrant tapestry of fractal mysticism, mandalas emerge as captivating enigmas, embodying the intricate dance between geometry and spirituality. These complex geometric configurations have not only enthralled the aesthetic senses of civilizations across the globe but also offered profound spiritual insights. This chapter delves into the fascinating realm where the precision of geometry and the depth of spirituality converge —mandalas.

The Geometric Symphony of Mandalas

Mandalas, derived from the ancient Sanskrit term for "circle," are more than mere circles; they are comprehensive visual representations of the universe's structure, embodying its vastness and complexity. They typically begin with a central point, representing the seed or essence of existence, from which an elaborate geometric matrix unfolds. This matrix is replete with intricate patterns, often comprising concentric circles, squares, and polygons that symbolize the cosmic order and the harmonious balance of the elements.

These geometric shapes are not random; they follow precise mathematical ratios and are imbued with specific symbolic meanings. For instance, the circle often represents wholeness and infinity, while the square symbolizes stability and groundedness. The interplay of these shapes within mandalas encapsulates the dynamic balance between the celestial and the terrestrial, the infinite and the finite, and the chaotic and the orderly.

Mandalas as Spiritual Portals

While the geometric intricacies of mandalas captivate the eyes, their true potency lies in their ability to function as spiritual portals. Mandalas serve as maps or blueprints for meditative practices across various traditions, guiding the seeker on an inward journey towards the center—the axis mundi or the spiritual core. This journey is not merely symbolic; it is an experiential traversal through layers of consciousness, mirroring the labyrinthine pathways of the mandala.

In Tibetan Buddhism, for instance, intricate sand mandalas are created with devout precision, each colored grain of sand placed with meditative focus. These mandalas are not only visual aids for meditation but also serve as reminders of the transient nature of existence; after their completion, they are dismantled, dispersing the sand to signify impermanence.

Mandalas in the Broader Cosmos

The paradigm of mandalas extends beyond human-made art; they are echoed in the grand fractal patterns that the cosmos etches across space and time. The spiral galaxies, the orbital paths of celestial bodies, and even the cyclonic patterns of weather systems reflect mandalic structures. They are omnipresent motifs in the fractal fabric of the universe, signifying the interconnectedness of all things and the cyclical nature of existence.

Furthermore, mandalas are not confined to the visual realm. The concept of a central point radiating outward into complex patterns can also be discerned in the acoustic domain—cymatics. When sound frequencies travel through a medium, they create geometric patterns reminiscent of mandalas, suggesting that the universe not only looks like a mandala but also resonates with mandalic harmony.

Conclusion

Mandalas are far more than artistic or spiritual curiosities; they are profound expressions of the fractal essence that pervades the cosmos. They encapsulate the mystical dance between order and chaos, simplicity and complexity, and the finite and the infinite. By exploring mandalas, one does not merely observe geometric patterns but engages with the fundamental principles that govern the universe, making them a pivotal subject in the study of fractal mysticism. As we progress further into the realms of sacred patterns, mandalas stand as a testament to the enchanting confluence of geometry and spirituality.

CHAPTER 16: QUANTUM CONNECTIONS

Venturing further into the captivating interplay between science and spirituality, Chapter 16 embarks on an exploration of the enigmatic world of quantum mechanics and its potential connections to fractal mysticism. Quantum physics, with its strange and counterintuitive phenomena, offers a fertile ground for examining the intricacies of the universe and the very fabric of reality. This chapter will delve into the confluence of quantum principles with fractal patterns and spirituality, inviting readers to contemplate the profound implications of this synergy.

Quantum Entanglement and Fractal Resonance

One of the most intriguing aspects of quantum physics is the phenomenon of entanglement, wherein particles become connected in such a way that the state of one instantly influences the state of the other, regardless of the distance separating them. This peculiar connection echoes the interconnectivity seen in fractal patterns, where each part reflects the whole, and the whole is inherent in each part. The concept of entanglement may offer a metaphorical parallel to the spiritual idea of oneness, where all is intertwined in an

CHAPTER 17: THE COMPLEXITY OF SIMPLICITY

In the fascinating journey through the realms of fractal mysticism, we have traversed the foundational landscapes of sacred geometry, chaos theory, and the spiritual significance of natural patterns. As we delve deeper into this intricate universe, we arrive at a pivotal juncture: the paradoxical relationship between simplicity and complexity, a theme that resonates profoundly within both fractal geometry and mystical traditions. This chapter endeavors to unravel this relationship, elucidating how simple mathematical rules can give rise to the elaborate tapestries of patterns that adorn both the natural world and the sacred spaces of our collective consciousness.

Simple Rules, Complex Worlds

At the heart of fractal geometry lies a startling revelation: the most complex and intricate patterns can emerge from the repetition of simple rules. This principle is vividly demonstrated in the formation of fractals, where a basic process, such as recursive division or iteration, when applied repeatedly, leads to structures of bewildering complexity. This phenomenon mirrors the mystical perspective that the universe, in all its vastness and intricacy, can be understood through the lens of thread is interwoven in a cosmic dance of chaos and order, matter and spirit, finitude and infinity. As we continue our journey through the chapters, we shall delve deeper into the complexities and wonders that arise from the sacred patterns of the universe.

mysticism acknowledges the coexistence of the material and the spiritual, the chaos and the order, the finite and the infinite. This duality is emblematic of the balance and harmony that fractal patterns and spiritual practices seek to achieve.

Quantum Tunneling and Transcendence

Quantum tunneling, where particles can pass through barriers that would be insurmountable in classical physics, evokes the mystical notion of transcendence. It is a metaphor for overcoming limitations and accessing higher states of consciousness, much like the way fractals transcend dimensions, existing between the lines of what is measurable and what is immeasurable. This transcendental aspect of quantum physics offers a scientific underpinning to the mystical pursuit of transcending the ordinary and reaching the extraordinary.

Implications and Contemplations

The profound parallels between quantum mechanics and fractal mysticism invite a reevaluation of our understanding of reality. The quantum connections underscore the possibility that the universe is far more interconnected and dynamic than previously imagined. They open up avenues for contemplating the nature of existence and the potential role of consciousness in shaping the fabric of the cosmos. By exploring these quantum connections, we find ourselves at the nexus of science and spirituality, where the mysteries of the universe unfold in fractal elegance.

In this chapter, we have only scratched the surface of the quantum realm and its mystical connotations. The insights gleaned from quantum physics and fractal patterns provide a glimpse into the enigmatic tapestry of reality, where every intricate web of existence, a reflection of the recursive nature of fractals.

Observer Effect and Consciousness

The observer effect in quantum mechanics posits that the act of observation can alter the state of a quantum system. This principle has led to various interpretations and speculations about the role of consciousness in shaping reality. In fractal mysticism, the notion that consciousness can influence or interact with the fundamental patterns of the universe is not unfamiliar. It suggests that, much like the recursive processes in fractals, the observer and the observed are part of a continuous feedback loop, intertwining the material and the spiritual.

Quantum Superposition and the Infinite

Quantum superposition, where a particle exists in all possible states simultaneously until it is observed, presents a striking resemblance to the infinite possibilities inherent in fractal geometry. Each branching in a fractal can be seen as a new possibility, an iteration that unfolds endlessly. Similarly, the superposition principle hints at a universe teeming with potentialities, where reality is not fixed but fluid and multifaceted. This multiplicity aligns with mystical traditions that embrace the infinite nature of the cosmos and the boundless potential of the spirit.

Wave-Particle Duality and Dual Nature of Reality

The wave-particle duality of quantum objects, where they exhibit both wave-like and particle-like properties, resonates with the dual nature of reality often described in mystical teachings. Just as light can be both a wave and a particle, fractal fundamental, universal laws. It is as though the cosmos, in its infinite wisdom, employs a minimalist approach, using a concise set of rules to paint the grand canvas of existence.

The Iterative Soul

Within the mystical traditions, there is often a focus on the practice of simple, repetitive rituals or mantras, which are believed to yield profound spiritual insights and transformations. This practice aligns with the iterative nature of fractal processes, where the act of repeating a simple pattern or formula leads to the emergence of a complex, infinitely varied structure. The parallel between fractal iteration and spiritual practice suggests a deep, underlying unity between the processes that govern the formation of natural patterns and the pathways to spiritual enlightenment.

Nature's Algorithm

The natural world is replete with examples of complex structures arising from simple rules. Consider the formation of snowflakes, each a unique masterpiece of symmetry and intricacy, all stemming from the simple, repetitive process of water molecules crystallizing in a hexagonal pattern. Similarly, the growth patterns of plants and trees, the branching of rivers, and the formation of mountain ranges all exemplify how nature employs straightforward algorithms to construct the rich tapestry of life on Earth. In this sense, nature itself can be seen as a fractal mystic, weaving complexity from the threads of simplicity.

In summary, this chapter has explored the profound interconnection between simplicity and complexity as exhibited in fractal geometry and mystical traditions. It has illuminated how simple rules, iteratively applied, are the genesis of the intricate and awe-inspiring patterns that permeate our universe, from the smallest snowflake to the vast cosmic web. This understanding offers a compelling perspective on the nature of reality, revealing that complexity need not arise from complexity; rather, it can unfold, with elegance and grace, from the simplest of beginnings. As we continue our exploration of fractal mysticism, we carry with us this profound insight, a guiding light in the quest to decipher the sacred patterns that bind the cosmos together.

CHAPTER 18: THE LORE OF LARGE NUMBERS

In the mystical odyssey of exploring fractals and the sacred patterns that permeate the cosmos, we've journeyed through the initial foundations of geometry, chaos, and the spiritual. Now, as we delve deeper into the intermediate realms of this enigmatic interlace, we arrive at a chapter devoted to a concept that is as mystifying as it is monumental: the lore of large numbers and their infinite sequences.

The Mystical Magnitude of Large Numbers: Large numbers hold a peculiar position in both the mathematical and mystical realms. They stretch beyond the ordinary, pushing the limits of comprehension and inviting awe and wonder. In various mystical traditions, large numbers often symbolize the vastness of the universe, the infinite nature of the divine, or the boundless extent of spiritual potential. Numerology, a mystical practice that interprets numbers' significance, attributes profound meanings to specific large numbers, seeing them as carriers of vibrational energy that resonate with cosmic forces.

From the esoteric teachings of Kabbalah, where numbers encode the very fabric of existence, to Hindu cosmology, which speaks of the colossal time scales of Yugas, large numbers have always captivated the human spirit. These grand scales and the figures that represent them aren't mere notations; they're windows to transcendence, glimpses into an infinite dance that choreographs the cosmos.

Infinite Sequences and Fractal Frontiers: The concept of infinity is intrinsically tied to large numbers. Infinite sequences, in particular, serve as the arteries through which the blood of fractal mysticism flows. These sequences are more than just endless lists of numbers; they're the rhythmic patterns that echo through fractal structures, the pulse of the recursive heartbeat.

Consider the iterative processes that shape the jagged coastline or the spirals in a galaxy; they are governed by infinite sequences that, despite their inherent simplicity, manifest in boundless complexity. These sequences are the mathematical mantras that repeat endlessly, weaving the fabric of reality into the intricate tapestry we observe in nature's fractals.

The Numina of Numerical Narratives: Numbers tell stories, narratives that transcend the pages of textbooks and permeate the metaphysical planes. The lore of large numbers and infinite sequences is a saga that unfolds in the liminal spaces between the known and the unknowable, between finite comprehension and the infinite cosmos.

In these numerical narratives, we find the Fibonacci sequence, where each number is the sum of the two preceding ones. This sequence is a refrain that repeats in the petal arrangements of flowers, the shells of snails, and even the proportions of the human body. It's a numerical narrative that whispers the secrets of growth, of life's unfolding patterns, and of the mystical connection between the microcosm and the macrocosm.

The Enigma of Eternity and the Endlessness of Numbers: Eternity has always been a concept that both mystics and mathematicians have grappled with. It's an idea that's as elusive as it is alluring. Large numbers and their infinite sequences provide a mathematical metaphor for eternity, a means to approach the unapproachable, to quantify the unquantifiable.

As we gaze into the vastness of numbers, where do we

find the line between the large and the infinite? Is there a point at which the addition of one more digit transcends the threshold of human comprehension and enters the realm of the eternal? These are questions that straddle the boundary between mathematics and mysticism, inviting contemplation and challenging our understanding of the very nature of existence.

In this chapter, we've explored the mystical significance of large numbers and infinite sequences, unraveling the narratives they weave and the sacred patterns they embody. Large numbers aren't just gargantuan figures; they're symbols of the limitless, the eternal, and the divine. They beckon us to expand our minds and spirits, to embrace the infinite fractal dance of the cosmos.

As we conclude this chapter, we carry with us the awe and reverence for the grandeur of numbers and the infinite sequences they spawn. They are the silent sentinels standing at the gates of eternity, the numerical narrators of the cosmos's most profound mysteries. In the chapters to come, we'll continue to traverse the complex tapestry of fractal mysticism, delving deeper into the sacred geometry that shapes our spiritual and material worlds.

CHAPTER 19: THE GOLDEN RATIO AND THE FIBONACCI SEQUENCE

In the realm of fractal mysticism, there exist numerical sequences and ratios that have captivated mathematicians, artists, and mystics alike for centuries. Among these, the Golden Ratio and the Fibonacci Sequence stand as titanic pillars, embodying a mysterious blend of mathematical precision and aesthetic beauty that resonates deeply within the patterns of the natural world and the esoteric principles of sacred geometry. This chapter delves into the profound significance of Phi, commonly known as the Golden Ratio, and the Fibonacci numbers in the context of fractal mysticism.

The Enigma of Phi: The Golden Ratio

The Golden Ratio, symbolized by the Greek letter Phi (Φ), is an irrational number approximately equal to 1.618033988749895. Its enigmatic quality lies in its unique property: if a line segment is divided into two parts, a and b, such that the whole length (a +b) is to the larger segment (a) as the larger segment (a) is to the smaller segment (b), the resulting ratio is always Phi. This self-similarity and recursion echo the essence of fractals, where the whole mirrors its parts in an endlessly repeating pattern.

Phi is not just a mathematical curiosity; it has been revered throughout history for its aesthetic properties. The Parthenon in Greece, Leonardo da Vinci's "Vitruvian Man," and even the pyramids of Egypt are all thought to incorporate the Golden Ratio in their design. This ubiquity in art and architecture may be attributed to its perceived beauty and balance, qualities that have not escaped the notice of those who seek deeper spiritual understanding through geometry.

In the realm of fractal mysticism, the Golden Ratio is seen as a divine proportion, a cosmic constant that resonates with the fabric of the universe. It symbolizes harmony, balance, and the intrinsic beauty of creation, often serving as a bridge between the material world and higher spiritual dimensions.

The Fibonacci Sequence: Numerical Harmony

The Fibonacci Sequence, a series of numbers where each number is the sum of the two preceding ones (0, 1, 1, 2, 3, 5, 8, 13, ...), holds a special place in the study of fractals and mysticism. Named after Leonardo of Pisa, known as Fibonacci, this sequence surfaces in various natural phenomena, from the branching of trees to the arrangement of leaves around a stem.

What ties the Fibonacci Sequence to the Golden Ratio is a fascinating convergence: as one progresses through the sequence, the ratio of consecutive numbers approaches Phi. This connection hints at a deeper, underlying order in the cosmos, a pattern woven into the very fabric of reality that resonates with the principles of fractal mysticism.

In spiritual traditions, the Fibonacci Sequence is often associated with growth, evolution, and the unfolding of life's mysteries. Each number is born from the sum of its predecessors, reflecting the idea of accumulation of knowledge and experience in the spiritual journey. The way the sequence approximates the Golden Ratio is seen as a reflection of the soul's progression towards divine harmony and enlightenment.

Fractals: The Dance of Numbers and Nature

The confluence of the Golden Ratio and the Fibonacci Sequence in fractals is a testament to the elegant complexity of the universe. Fractals, with their self-similar patterns, embody these mathematical principles in a stunning display of visual harmony. The branching of trees, the spiral arrangements of galaxies, and even the human cardiovascular system are all fractal in nature and exhibit properties related to Phi and the Fibonacci numbers.

In fractal mysticism, these patterns are not mere coincidences but are considered sacred codes, cosmic fingerprints of the divine. They serve as reminders that the universe is intricately ordered and that this order is accessible through the study of geometry and numbers. The recursive nature of fractals echoes the spiritual journey, where each step is both a repetition and an expansion of what came before, leading to infinite growth and understanding.

Conclusion

The Golden Ratio and the Fibonacci Sequence, woven into the tapestry of the universe, stand as powerful symbols of the interconnectedness between mathematics, nature, and spirituality. Their presence in fractals offers a glimpse into the profound order that underlies the chaos of existence, providing a pathway for mystical contemplation and insight. As we unravel the mysteries of these sacred patterns, we inch closer to understanding the geometry of the divine, a journey that spans the macrocosm of galaxies to the microcosm of our own DNA.

In the next chapter, we will venture into the realm of

non-Euclidean spaces and explore their spiritual implications, further expanding our understanding of the mystical geometries that shape our universe.

CHAPTER 20: NON-EUCLIDEAN SPACES

The familiar and intuitive geometry of Euclidean spaces, with its straight lines, right angles, and circles, constitutes the bedrock of our everyday experience. Yet, the mathematical universe extends beyond the realms of the familiar, venturing into the enigmatic landscapes of Non-Euclidean spaces. These spaces, which eschew the postulates of Euclid in favor of their unique axioms, offer a profound insight into the convolutions of the cosmos, the nature of reality, and the potential gateways to mystical experiences.

The Non-Euclidean Revelation

Non-Euclidean geometries, primarily hyperbolic and spherical, emerge when one or more of Euclid's original axioms are altered or negated. In spherical geometry, for instance, straight lines are redefined as great circles, like the equator on a globe, and parallel lines do not exist, as all lines eventually converge. Hyperbolic geometry, on the other hand, is characterized by saddle-shaped surfaces where the Euclidean parallel postulate is replaced by the stipulation that through a point not on a line, infinite lines can be drawn parallel to the original line.

These geometries, once purely theoretical constructs, have found tangible manifestations in the natural world and have significantly impacted our understanding of the universe. The curvature of space-time, as postulated by Einstein's General Theory of Relativity, is an embodiment of non-Euclidean geometry, demonstrating that the very fabric of the cosmos is woven with hyperbolic threads.

Spiritual Implications of Non-Euclidean Spaces

The transcendence of Non-Euclidean spaces over traditional, linear confines offers a tantalizing parallel to spiritual journeys that seek to transcend the limitations of conventional reality. Just as spherical geometry redefines the nature of parallel lines and proximity, mystic traditions frequently challenge and redefine the concepts of time, proximity, and connection, often proposing that all beings and events are intricately and intimately connected beyond the visible.

In hyperbolic geometry, with its infinite parallel lines through a single point, one might find a symbolic representation of the infinite potentialities, paths, and realities that mystic traditions suggest. This plurality of paths echoes the spiritual notion that there are countless routes to enlightenment or spiritual fulfillment, each tailored to the individual soul's journey.

Non-Euclidean Spaces and Altered States of Consciousness

Mystical experiences often involve altered states of consciousness where the constraints of time, space, and identity dissolve. In such states, the linear, Euclidean perception of the world gives way to a more fluid and dynamic understanding. The boundless horizons of Non-Euclidean spaces serve as a powerful metaphor for these altered states, where the soul roams free, unbound by the rigid frameworks of ordinary perception.

The intricate patterns of hyperbolic crochet or the spherical panoramas of planetarium domes can elicit a visceral understanding of these geometries, offering glimpses into the profound and often bewildering experiences reported by mystics. These experiences, much like the journey through Non-Euclidean spaces, invite the seeker to embrace complexity, to find comfort in ambiguity, and to recognize the inherent interconnectedness of all things.

In summary, the exploration of Non-Euclidean spaces serves not only as an intellectual exercise but also as a spiritual pilgrimage. It invites us to reconsider the nature of reality, to challenge our assumptions, and to open ourselves to the profound interconnectedness that underlies the cosmos. As we journey through these enigmatic landscapes, we gain a deeper appreciation for the mystical journey itself, recognizing that the path to enlightenment, much like Non-Euclidean geometry, is not always straight, but always profoundly transformative.

CHAPTER 21: THE HIDDEN DIMENSIONS

The universe, an enigmatic cosmos, whispers its secrets in a language of mathematics, geometry, and vibrations. Among the most mystifying and alluring of these secrets are the theories that propose the existence of hidden dimensions beyond the familiar three-dimensional space. This chapter delves into the intricate theories surrounding these hidden dimensions and their profound mystical significance.

Unveiling the Veiled: Higher Dimensional Theories

The concept of dimensions beyond the perceivable three has tantalized mathematicians, physicists, and mystics alike. In the realm of theoretical physics, string theory and M-theory postulate the existence of multiple dimensions beyond the observable universe. String theory suggests the existence of at least ten dimensions, while M-theory posits eleven. These dimensions aren't simply extensions of space but are woven into the fundamental fabric of reality, shaping the universe in ways that are imperceptible yet vital to its very existence.

The mystics, on the other hand, have long intuited the presence of these hidden realms, often interpreting them as spiritual planes or levels of consciousness. These higher dimensions are said to be realms of profound wisdom and enlightenment, where the physical laws of the lower dimensions give way to the subtler, more flexible laws of spirit and light.

The Interdimensional Loom: Weaving the Spiritual with the Physical

The hidden dimensions are believed to serve as the bridge between the tangible and intangible, the physical and spiritual. In fractal mysticism, these dimensions are the higher iterations of reality, where the fractal nature of the universe expresses itself in increasingly complex and beautiful ways.

Each higher dimension adds a layer of complexity and depth to the fractal patterns that permeate the cosmos. Just as a two-dimensional fractal pattern can be extended into the third dimension to create a more intricate structure, so too can the patterns of our three-dimensional world be extended into these higher realms, creating a tapestry of spiritual and physical interconnectedness.

The Mystical Significance of Hidden Dimensions

The mystical significance of these hidden dimensions lies in their representation of the deeper, more esoteric aspects of existence. They are often associated with states of higher consciousness, transcendence, and the attainment of spiritual wisdom. In many mystical traditions, the journey through these dimensions is akin to the soul's ascent, a path of spiritual evolution and enlightenment.

These dimensions are also seen as the abode of divine entities and higher beings, with each dimension resonating at a different vibrational frequency. The higher the dimension, the more refined and spiritually elevated the vibration, culminating in the ultimate unity with the source, the divine, or the infinite.

In conclusion, the hidden dimensions stand as a testament

to the universe's boundless complexity and the interwoven nature of the physical and spiritual realms. They challenge our perceptions and invite us to expand our understanding of reality, leading us on a journey of discovery that transcends the confines of our three-dimensional existence. As we explore these enigmatic dimensions, we unravel the mystical threads that connect us to the greater cosmos, finding harmony in the geometry of the divine.

CHAPTER 22: TIME, FRACTALS, AND ETERNITY

The intrinsic nature of time has perplexed philosophers, mystics, and scientists for millennia. Is it linear, cyclical, or an illusion altogether? In this chapter, we delve into the profound connections between the temporal tapestry of existence and the fractal geometry that underpins the cosmos. We explore how fractals offer a unique lens through which to perceive the cyclical and eternal aspects of time, bridging the mystical with the mathematical in an intricate dance of infinity.

The Fractal Nature of Time

Imagine time not as a straight line, but as a spiraling fractal, continuously looping and curving back upon itself. This concept posits that moments are not isolated instances but interwoven segments of a grander, self-similar pattern. Such a fractal representation aligns with many spiritual traditions that view time as cyclical, characterized by recurring ages, seasons, and life cycles.

Consider, for instance, the ancient Hindu concept of Yugas, vast epochs of time that repeat in a cyclical fashion, each containing the seeds of its own end and rebirth. Similarly, the Mayan calendar with its intricate cycles and the Ouroboros, the ancient symbol of a serpent eating its own tail, signify the eternal return and the fractal-like nature of time. These symbols and beliefs echo the recursive properties of fractals, where each cycle is a self-similar iteration of the last, differing only in scale.

Fractals and the Illusion of Linearity

Our conventional understanding of time is largely linear. We perceive it as a straight arrow, propelling us from the past, through the present, and into the future. However, fractal geometry challenges this notion by illustrating that linearity is but a narrow view of a much richer tapestry. Just as fractals reveal complexity in apparent simplicity, they invite us to reconsider time as a multifaceted, dimensional entity.

In fractal patterns, each fragment holds the essence of the whole, suggesting that each moment in time encapsulates the entirety of existence. Thus, past, present, and future may not be distinct entities but different expressions of the same underlying reality. This resonates with mystical experiences where individuals report a transcendence of linear time, encountering the past and future as a simultaneous, interconnected whole.

Eternity Within the Temporal

If time is fractal, then the concept of eternity gains a new dimension. Eternity is often seen as an infinite extension of time, a never-ending line stretching into the void. However, through the fractal lens, eternity is not about endless duration but about depth and interconnectedness. Each moment contains within it the seeds of infinity, mirroring the recursive nature of fractals where each part reflects the whole.

This perspective aligns with the mystical notion that the eternal can be found within the transient, that the sacred is hidden within the mundane. In moments of profound spiritual insight, the barriers of time dissolve, and one glimpses the eternal "now" that is the heart of all existence.

Implications for Spiritual Practice

Understanding time as a fractal has profound implications for spiritual practice. It suggests a shift from a linear progression toward enlightenment to a recognition of the sacredness inherent in each moment. Spiritual growth, then, is not about reaching a distant goal but about deepening one's awareness of the fractal, eternal nature of the present.

Meditative practices, for instance, often focus on the present moment, inviting practitioners to experience the depth and fullness of the "now." This is akin to zooming into a fractal, discovering ever more intricate patterns within each iteration. Such practices help dissolve the illusion of linear time, revealing the timeless essence that underlies our temporal experience.

In conclusion, the intersection of time, fractals, and eternity offers a rich tapestry of insights into the nature of existence. By envisioning time as a fractal spiral, we open ourselves to a world where the linear is embraced by the cyclical, where each moment is a microcosm of eternity. This perspective not only bridges science and mysticism but also invites us into a deeper engagement with the sacredness of the temporal world. As we explore the fractal dimensions of time, we uncover the eternal dance of chaos and order, a dance in which we are all intimately entwined.

CHAPTER 23: THE MYSTICAL UNIVERSE AS A HOLOGRAM

Diving into the concept of the universe as a hologram requires an audacious suspension of conventional perceptions, challenging us to contemplate existence in a manner radically divergent from traditional viewpoints. The holographic principle, an idea that extends beyond the frontiers of ordinary understanding, postulates that the entire universe can be envisaged as a two-dimensional information structure "painted" on the cosmological horizon, such that the three dimensions we observe are merely an effective description at macroscopic scales and low energies.

The Holographic Principle: Unraveling the Fabric of Reality

At the heart of the holographic universe theory lies the holographic principle, a tenet which arose from black hole thermodynamics and string theory. In essence, the principle suggests that the information contained within a volume of space can be represented on a boundary to that space – akin to a holographic image. This implies a staggering possibility: that our perceived three-dimensional reality is but a holographic projection of information encoded on a distant, two-dimensional surface.

Theoretical physicist Leonard Susskind was a pioneer in formulating this principle, inspired by the work of physicist Jacob Bekenstein and the enigmatic properties of black holes. The idea that the information content of all the objects that have fallen into a black hole could be entirely contained in surface fluctuations of the event horizon challenges our intuitive understanding of reality and propels us into a realm where the fabric of space-time is interwoven with the threads of information.

Fractal Geometry: The Recursive Nature of the Cosmos

Fractal geometry, characterized by self-similar patterns recurring at progressively smaller scales, provides a mathematical framework for the holographic principle. If the universe can indeed be described holographically, then like a fractal, the macroscopic patterns we observe are reflections of microscopic dynamics. The Mandelbrot set, an emblem of fractal mathematics, is a quintessential example where an infinitude of complexity arises from simple rules – a notion mirrored in the concept of a holographic universe.

This perspective positions every fragment of the universe as a microcosm of the whole, reflecting the ancient Hermetic aphorism, "As above, so below." In the holographic universe, this axiom finds not only philosophical but also scientific resonance, as the macrocosmic expanse of the cosmos is reflected in the microcosmic depths of subatomic particles.

Mystical Implications: A Universe Interconnected

The holographic model of the universe resonates deeply with mystical traditions, which have long espoused the interconnectedness of all things. In various esoteric teachings, the notion that each part contains the whole is a recurrent theme. The holographic principle provides a scientific scaffold for these mystical insights, suggesting that each point in space-time could contain the information for the entire universe.

This intertwining of science and mysticism opens the door to profound contemplation about the nature of consciousness, reality, and the divine. In many mystical traditions, the concept of non-duality—that the observer and the observed are one—is a cornerstone. The holographic universe presents a paradigm where the separation between observer and observed blurs, where each observer is potentially a reflection of the entire cosmos, and where consciousness itself might be understood as an emergent phenomenon from the fundamental holographic fabric of reality.

In contemplating the universe as a hologram, we are ushered into a domain where the boundaries between science, philosophy, and mysticism dissolve into a unified tapestry of understanding. The holographic principle, while grounded in the rigorous mathematics of black hole thermodynamics and string theory, echoes the perennial wisdom of mystics who have long perceived the universe as an intricate, interconnected web of existence. As we ponder our place within this fractal hologram, we find ourselves at the nexus of infinity, beholding a cosmos more wondrous and enigmatic than we could have ever imagined.

CHAPTER 24: CELLULAR AUTOMATA AND SPIRITUAL MODELS

At the heart of fractal mysticism lies an intriguing parallelism between the digital realm of computational models and the intricate tapestry of spiritual beliefs. Cellular automata, simple yet profound in their execution, serve as a quintessential bridge between these two seemingly disparate worlds. This chapter delves into the profound implications of cellular automata for spiritual models, exploring how these computational systems offer profound insights into the mystical principles that underpin the universe.

Cellular Automata: The Computational Microcosm

Cellular automata are discrete, grid-based computational systems, where each cell in the grid follows a set of rules to determine its state based on the states of neighboring cells. At the core of cellular automata is the concept of iteration—a process that echoes the recursive nature of fractals. Cellular automata are known for their ability to generate complex patterns from simple rules, a property that resonates deeply with the fractal mysticism's emphasis on the emergence of complexity from simplicity.

One of the most well-known cellular automata is Conway's Game of Life, a simulation that demonstrates how life-like properties such as birth, death, and survival can emerge from simple binary rules. Despite its simplicity, the Game of Life encapsulates a universe of possibilities, leading to patterns that are remarkably reminiscent of organic growth and decay. This resemblance is not lost on those who study fractal mysticism, for it suggests a computational mirror to the cycles of life and death, growth and decay, that permeate the natural world.

Spiritual Archetypes in Cellular Automata

The patterns that emerge in cellular automata often bear a striking resemblance to archetypal spiritual symbols. Spirals, gliders, and oscillators that arise within these systems can be seen as digital counterparts to mandalas, the eternal dance of Shiva, or the rhythmic cycles of creation and destruction found in numerous spiritual traditions. These patterns, governed by deterministic rules, evoke a sense of cosmic order—a reassurance that beneath the chaos of existence, there is an underlying structure, an algorithmic divinity that choreographs the dance of the cosmos.

Cellular Automata and the Illusion of Free Will

A profound question arises when one ponders cellular automata in the context of spirituality: If the universe is akin to a grand computational system, where does that leave the concept of free will? In many spiritual traditions, free will is a cornerstone, an essential aspect of the human experience. Yet, the deterministic nature of cellular automata challenges this notion, suggesting a universe where everything is preordained by immutable laws.

However, it is within the unpredictable outcomes of simple rules that a reconciliation can be found. Just as cellular automata can generate unforeseeable complexity, so too can the universe surprise us, rendering the future a tapestry woven from both determinism and chance. In this light, free will can be seen as the conscious navigation through a probabilistic landscape sculpted by cosmic rules.

The Spiritual Significance of Emergence

Emergence, the process through which complex systems arise from simple interactions, is a cornerstone of cellular automata. This phenomenon bears significant spiritual implications, as it reflects the mystic belief in the interconnectedness of all things. In fractal mysticism, the macrocosm is a reflection of the microcosm, and vice versa. Cellular automata exemplify this principle, showing how localized, simple interactions can give rise to global, complex behaviors that seem to transcend the sum of their parts.

This emergent behavior is akin to the spiritual quest for enlightenment or awakening—a journey where incremental, often mundane, experiences and realizations culminate in a profound transformation. Just as a seemingly insignificant cell in a cellular automaton can influence the emergence of a complex pattern, so too can small, personal spiritual practices contribute to the awakening of consciousness.

Concluding Reflections

In exploring cellular automata, we find a digital microcosm that mirrors the spiritual macrocosm. These computational models serve as a modern parable for the mystical principles that pervade the universe, encapsulating the emergence of complexity from simplicity, the balance of determinism and chance, and the interconnectedness of all things. Cellular automata remind us that within the grids of our existence, whether digital or spiritual, lies the potential for infinite complexity and beauty—an ode to the fractal nature of the cosmos.

As we close this chapter, we are left with a renewed appreciation for the profound symmetry between the computational and the spiritual. Cellular automata stand as testament to the universe's ability to generate boundless complexity from the simplest of rules—a concept that resonates at the core of fractal mysticism.

CHAPTER 25: VIBRATIONAL FREQUENCY AND RESONANCE

Harmonics, frequencies, resonances — these are not just the lingua franca of the scientist, but also the mystic. In this chapter, we delve into the mystical dimension of vibrations, exploring their ubiquitous presence from the macrocosm of celestial mechanics to the microcosm of subatomic fluctuations, unraveling their role in the grand symphony of existence.

The Symphony of the Cosmos

The cosmos is often likened to a grand symphony, with each celestial body contributing its own unique note to the cosmic orchestra. This metaphor finds its grounding in the fact that every object in the universe, from the smallest particle to the largest galaxy, is in constant vibrational motion. Each vibration carries a specific frequency, an oscillation that is as unique to the object as a fingerprint is to a human being.

In the mystical traditions, these cosmic vibrations are not merely physical phenomena. They embody the very essence of life and spirituality. The frequency of an object is seen as a direct manifestation of its inherent nature, its spiritual 'DNA' so to speak. This concept is epitomized in the ancient Hindu philosophy of Nāda Yoga, where the universe's creation is attributed to the primordial sound "Om," the original vibration from which all existence emanates.

Resonance: The Dance of Sympathetic Vibrations

Resonance occurs when one object vibrating at a certain frequency induces a vibrational response in another object. In the physical world, this is observed when a singer's voice can shatter a glass or when an army breaks step while crossing a bridge to avoid a resonant disaster. In spirituality, resonance is the underpinning principle of connectedness. The concept of 'sympathetic vibrations' extends beyond physical mechanics into the realm of human consciousness and relationships. It is the resonance that is felt when individuals are 'on the same wavelength,' or when a particular place or piece of music 'resonates' with someone on a deeper, often inexplicable, level.

Frequency and Healing: The Therapeutic Note

The intersection of vibrational frequencies and mysticism is not solely confined to abstract concepts but has practical implications in the domain of healing. Various healing traditions, including Reiki and sound therapy, assert that disease is a manifestation of disharmony in the body's vibrational frequencies. By introducing sounds or vibrations that resonate with the natural frequencies of the body, practitioners believe they can restore balance and promote healing. Tibetan singing bowls, tuning forks, and even the human voice are employed as instruments to recalibrate the body's frequencies. While empirical research into these practices is ongoing, numerous anecdotal accounts speak to their transformative potential.

The Resonant Universe

Quantum physics has given credence to the mystical idea that everything is interconnected through the concept of quantum entanglement. This phenomenon, often described as 'spooky action at a distance,' implies that particles can become linked in such a way that the state of one instantaneously influences the state of the other, regardless of distance. This quantum interconnectedness echoes the mystical belief in the resonance of all things, suggesting that the vibrations of one entity can influence the vibrations of another, across vast stretches of space and time.

In our journey through the chapters of this book, we have traversed various landscapes of thought and spirit. In this exploration of vibrational frequency and resonance, we find a unifying thread — a harmonic convergence of science and spirituality. The vibrational nature of the universe is not merely a physical phenomenon to be measured and quantified, but a mystical reality to be experienced and revered. As we attune ourselves to the vibrations around us, we tune into the deeper resonances of existence, finding harmony in the cosmic symphony that plays eternally in the background of our lives.

CHAPTER 26: THE MANDELBROT SET AND THE GEOMETRY OF THE DIVINE

The Mandelbrot Set is an emblem of mathematical enigma and aesthetic wonder, a staple in the pantheon of fractal geometry. But what does this seemingly abstract construct have to do with the sacred and the divine? This chapter delves deep into the Mandelbrot Set's mystical implications, exploring its transcendental quality and its metaphorical resonance with the infinite and the divine.

The Mandelbrot Set: A Portal to Infinity

At its core, the Mandelbrot Set is generated by a simple mathematical formula iterated over complex numbers. Yet, this iterative process gives rise to an infinitely complex boundary—a fractal frontier that neither repeats nor ends. This boundary dances tantalizingly close to the concept of infinity, a notion that has traditionally been ascribed to the divine. In many mystical traditions, the divine is seen as boundless, infinite, and unfathomable—qualities that the Mandelbrot Set seems to visually manifest.

Metaphors of Creation

The creation stories of various cultures speak of the world being formed from chaos, a primordial soup of potential. Interestingly, the Mandelbrot Set itself emerges from the complex plane's chaotic sea, manifesting as a coherent structure, an island of stability amidst the turbulent waves of divergence. This can be seen as a metaphor for the divine act of creation, where order is born from chaos, and form emerges from formlessness. The Mandelbrot Set's infinitely repeating patterns, scaling down to ever-smaller scales, can be interpreted as a mathematical model of the principle of "as above, so below," which suggests that the macrocosm is reflected in the microcosm—a key tenet in various mystical traditions.

The Mandelbrot Set and the Human Psyche

The Mandelbrot Set's intricacy and complexity mirror the complexities of the human psyche, with its infinite layers, paradoxes, and recursions. Just as the Mandelbrot Set holds infinitely nested variations within its bounds, so too does the human mind harbor endless depths of thoughts, emotions, and consciousness. In this sense, the Mandelbrot Set can be viewed as a symbolic representation of the human soul—a fractal tapestry woven from the threads of our inner experiences, where every part contains the whole.

Symbolism of the Mandelbrot Set

The Mandelbrot Set is rich in symbolism. Its shape, reminiscent of a heart, a Buddhist Stupa, or even a fetal figure, invites interpretations across various mystical and religious traditions. It is as if the Mandelbrot Set acts as a Rorschach inkblot, reflecting the viewer's innermost spiritual beliefs and understandings. The boundary of the Mandelbrot Set, forever approaching but never quite reaching perfect repetition, symbolizes the spiritual journey—an eternal approach towards the divine, towards enlightenment, but never quite reaching it in this plane of existence.

Conclusion

The Mandelbrot Set is not merely a mathematical curiosity; it is a profound symbol, a mirror reflecting our own infinite nature and the boundless intricacies of the divine. It reminds us that within the seemingly mundane equations and numbers lies a gateway to the infinite, a path that leads us closer to the ultimate understanding of the cosmos and our place within it. The Mandelbrot Set and the Geometry of the Divine is a testament to the profound connection between mathematics, mysticism, and the sacred patterns woven into the very fabric of reality.

CHAPTER 27: PARADOXES AND SELF-REFERENCE

In the intricate tapestry of fractal mysticism, paradoxes and self-reference serve as the warp and weft, interlacing the tangible with the ethereal, the comprehensible with the enigmatic. This chapter delves into the mystical role of these elements within fractal structures and teachings, navigating the labyrinthine corridors of paradoxical thought and recursive patterns, uncovering the magic that resides in the complexity of simplicity.

The Lure of the Labyrinth: Paradoxes in Fractal Mysticism

Paradoxes, those seemingly absurd or self-contradictory statements or propositions that, upon closer inspection, reveal an underlying truth, have long fascinated mystics and mathematicians alike. In the realm of fractal mysticism, paradoxes are not just curiosities to ponder but are fundamental to understanding the inherent nature of the universe. They serve as keys to unlock deeper metaphysical truths, revealing the liminal spaces where logic melds with intuition.

One such paradox is the famous "Menger Sponge," a fractal object that is a three-dimensional paradox in itself. It is a geometric shape that, when its iterative process is carried to infinity, results in a structure that has an infinite surface area but zero volume. This paradoxical nature echoes the mystical teachings of various traditions, which often speak of the unity between the infinite and the finite, the material and the immaterial.

The Ouroboros: Self-Reference and Recursion

Self-reference, a concept where a statement or formula refers back to itself, is another cornerstone of fractal mysticism. It is exemplified in the image of the Ouroboros, the ancient symbol of a serpent eating its own tail, representing the cyclical nature of existence, the eternal return, and the unity of all things.

In fractals, self-reference manifests as recursion, the process where a pattern repeats itself at progressively smaller scales. This recursive property is not just a mathematical curiosity but a profound reflection of the universe's structure. The Mandelbrot set, perhaps the most famous fractal, is a testament to the power of self-reference. Each minuscule part of this set, when magnified, reveals a complexity and structure similar to the whole, a characteristic that resonates with mystical teachings about the holographic nature of reality.

The Enigma of Infinity

Paradoxes and self-reference in fractal mysticism inevitably lead to contemplations on the concept of infinity. Infinity, a concept that has perplexed and intrigued humanity since time immemorial, is intrinsic to fractals. The infinitely repeating patterns, the boundless iterations, and the unfathomable depths of fractal structures reflect the mystical understanding of the infinite nature of the cosmos and the divine.

The enigma of infinity is most poignantly expressed in the paradoxical question, "What happens when an unstoppable force meets an immovable object?" This conundrum echoes in fractal mysticism's exploration of the infinite, where the boundaries of logic are stretched, and the mind is invited to transcend its finite constraints.

In conclusion, this chapter has navigated the serpentine paths of paradoxes and self-reference, key elements that bind the mystical tapestry of fractals. Through exploring the Menger Sponge, the Ouroboros, and the conundrums of infinity, we have glimpsed the profound connections between fractal geometry and mystical teachings, where the paradoxical and the recursive not only coexist but illuminate the enigmatic beauty of the cosmos.

CHAPTER 28: RANDOMNESS AND DETERMINISM

At the heart of fractal mysticism lies an intriguing dichotomy: the interplay between randomness and determinism. This chapter delves into the realms of unpredictability and predetermined patterns, both of which are central to understanding the nature of fractals and their relation to spiritual beliefs. By navigating through the complex relationship between these concepts, we unravel how they reflect the intricate balance in the universe and in our spiritual understanding of it.

The Essence of Randomness in Fractals

Randomness, often perceived as a lack of order or predictability, plays a pivotal role in the formation of fractal patterns. In nature, we observe random processes contributing to the intricate beauty of fractals. The unpredictable path of a lightning bolt, the irregular branching of trees, or the complex coastline shaped by numerous environmental factors —all exhibit an element of randomness. In the mystical context, randomness is seen as the divine play, or 'Lila', a concept in Eastern spiritual traditions where the universe is created out of a divine sense of spontaneity and playfulness.

Randomness is not devoid of rules, however. It operates within certain boundaries, which leads to the emergence of patterns. This is where the interplay with determinism becomes apparent. Deterministic systems, governed by specific rules or laws, can give rise to complex and seemingly random structures. The deterministic nature of such systems is crucial in the formation of fractals, where simple, repeating processes lead to infinitely complex patterns.

The Deterministic Underpinnings

Determinism holds that all events are determined by pre-existing causes. In fractal geometry, deterministic processes often manifest in the form of iteration—a repetitive application of a simple rule. The iconic Mandelbrot Set, for instance, arises from iterating a simple mathematical equation. Despite its deterministic foundation, the resulting pattern exhibits infinite complexity and variation, qualities often associated with randomness.

In mystical traditions, determinism is paralleled in the concept of destiny or fate. Many spiritual beliefs hold that the universe operates according to a divine plan, a predetermined course that guides the evolution of the cosmos and the lives within it. However, within this apparent predestination, there is room for random events and free will, reflecting the balance between determinism and randomness.

Navigating the Balance

The relationship between randomness and determinism is not just a philosophical pondering but has practical implications in understanding the universe and our place in it. The interplay between these forces mirrors the balance found in the spiritual journey. Just as fractals are shaped by both random events and deterministic rules, our lives are influenced by a combination of chance encounters and the structured paths we follow.

In many spiritual practices, this balance is embraced. For instance, divination systems like the I Ching or Tarot rely on random elements (the casting of coins or drawing of cards) interpreted through a deterministic framework of symbolism and meaning. In these practices, randomness is not seen as mere chaos, but as a doorway to deeper insights and a reflection of the mysterious interplay of forces in the universe.

In conclusion, the dance between randomness and determinism in fractal mysticism mirrors the complex interplay of chaos and order in the universe. Through understanding fractals, we gain insight into the nature of reality, where randomness and determinism are not opposing forces but complementary aspects of a unified whole. This chapter invites us to contemplate the beauty and intricacy of this balance, encouraging us to reflect on how it manifests in the natural world, in the mystical traditions, and in the very fabric of our existence.

CHAPTER 29: CRYSTALLOGRAPHY AND SPIRITUAL LATTICES

In this chapter, we delve into the mesmerizing realm of crystallography and explore its profound implications in the context of fractal mysticism. Crystals, with their ordered structures and inherent symmetry, serve as a tangible representation of the harmony and balance that many spiritual traditions seek to understand and embody. The lattice structures of crystals, much like the intricate patterns we observe in fractals, manifest the interplay of chaos and order, revealing a hidden script of the universe that resonates with mystical significance.

Subtle Symmetries and Sacred Structures

At the heart of crystallography lies the study of symmetry and lattice structures, the foundational elements that govern the formation and properties of crystals. The geometric perfection inherent in these natural formations has long captured the human imagination, evoking a sense of the divine. In various mystical traditions, crystals are revered not only for their physical beauty but also for their purported metaphysical properties. The precise and repetitive patterns observed in crystal lattices are reminiscent of the recursive nature of fractals, where simplicity begets complexity.

These lattices are not mere physical constructs; they are symbolic of the underlying order that permeates the cosmos. In the intricate dance of atoms and molecules arranging themselves into crystalline structures, one can discern a metaphor for the cosmic order—an interplay of forces and energies that shape the very fabric of existence. This order is not rigid but dynamic, much like the evolving patterns of fractals, reflecting the ebb and flow of the universal life force that many spiritual paths recognize.

Crystalline Consciousness: Metaphors of Growth and Transformation

Beyond their physical allure, crystals have been imbued with rich spiritual symbolism, reflecting themes of growth, transformation, and enlightenment. The process of crystallization, a transition from chaos to order, mirrors the spiritual journey of the soul as it seeks to align with the fundamental patterns of the universe. This journey is not unlike the iterative process that generates fractals, where each step brings one closer to the infinite complexity and beauty of the whole.

In the context of fractal mysticism, crystals serve as potent metaphors for the soul's evolution. Just as crystals grow layer by layer, adding to their structure while maintaining their inherent symmetry, the spiritual seeker incrementally acquires wisdom and understanding, expanding their consciousness while remaining grounded in the eternal truths that the crystal lattice epitomizes.

The Resonance of Crystalline Networks

Crystals also exemplify the concept of resonance, a principle that holds significant sway in both the scientific and spiritual domains. The lattice structure of a crystal enables it to resonate at specific frequencies, a phenomenon that has practical applications in technology and has also been metaphorically extended to the spiritual domain. In many esoteric teachings, the resonance of crystals is believed to align with the vibrational frequencies of the human body and spirit, facilitating healing and spiritual attunement.

This idea of resonance finds a parallel in fractal mysticism, where the recursive patterns are seen as resonating with the fundamental frequencies of the universe. The fractal nature of reality suggests that the same patterns repeat at various scales, creating a symphony of cosmic resonance that the spiritually attuned individual can perceive and harmonize with.

In summary, the study of crystallography opens up new dimensions in our understanding of fractal mysticism. The ordered beauty of crystal lattices resonates deeply with the principles of sacred geometry and the mystical pursuit of understanding the patterns that underlie our reality. As we contemplate the crystalline structures that abound in nature, we are reminded of the intricate tapestry of existence—a tapestry woven with the threads of chaos and order, simplicity and complexity, reflecting the infinite creativity of the universe.

CHAPTER 30: THE ZENO PHENOMENON AND INFINITE REDUCTION

The allure of the infinite has perpetually captivated the human imagination, invoking a sense of wonder and, at times, existential trepidation. The very concept of infinity manifests itself not only in the expansive cosmos but also in the infinitely minute, an idea poignantly encapsulated in the Zeno Phenomenon. This chapter delves into the profundities of infinite reduction, exploring its spiritual implications and its entwining with the mystical.

The Dichotomy of Zeno's Paradoxes

Zeno of Elea, an ancient philosopher, proposed several paradoxes that challenge our comprehension of motion, space, and time. Central to our discussion is the "Dichotomy Paradox," which posits that before an object can traverse a certain distance, it must first cover half that distance. However, to cover that half, it must first cross a quarter, and before a quarter, an eighth, and so on ad infinitum. This infinite regression implies that motion is an illusion, a startling conclusion that resonates with certain mystical traditions, which posit that the material world is an illusion, a Maya, veiling a more profound and boundless reality.

The Infinite in Fractal Geometry

Fractals are embodiments of infinity. They can be magnified endlessly, revealing ceaselessly intricate patterns, akin to the infinite division proposed by Zeno's paradox. This notion of a never-ending descent into the microscopic realms of reality invites contemplation on the nature of the divine. In many mystical traditions, the divine is conceived as boundless and ineffable, an infinite source manifesting through the finite forms of the cosmos. In fractal geometry, we witness a mathematical parallel to this spiritual principle, where each fragment, no matter how minute, encapsulates the whole.

The Spiritual Interpretation of Infinite Reduction

In spiritual discourse, the journey inward is often framed as a path towards enlightenment or divine union. The Zeno Phenomenon, interpreted mystically, becomes a metaphor for this inward journey, where each layer of the self that is peeled back reveals a deeper, more authentic layer. This infinite introspection parallels the infinite complexity of fractals and reflects a mystical understanding of the soul's journey: an endless sojourn towards the core of one's being, where the universal and the individual converge.

Quantum Connections: The Infinite in the Infinitesimal

The quantum realm, with its probabilities and indeterminacies, echoes the perplexities of the Zeno Phenomenon. The act of observing a quantum event changes the event itself, a conundrum reminiscent of the paradoxical nature of motion in Zeno's dichotomy. Furthermore, quantum entanglement, where particles remain interconnected regardless of distance, introduces a level of unity that transcends spatial limitations. This unity resonates with the mystical notion of the oneness of all creation, a oneness that persists whether one examines the macrocosm or delves into the microcosm.

Conclusion

The Zeno Phenomenon, with its paradoxical essence and its flirtation with the infinite, provides a rich substrate for mystical contemplation. It challenges our perceptions of reality and propels us to ponder the infinite in both the cosmic and the quantum. Fractal mysticism, in embracing the infinite reduction, serves as a bridge between the tangible and the transcendent, between the known and the ineffable. In this intricate dance between chaos and order, between finitude and infinity, we catch glimpses of the divine geometry that orchestrates the universe—a geometry that beckons us to look beyond the surface and embrace the boundless mystery enshrouded within the finite.

CHAPTER 31: INTERSECTION OF FRACTALS AND ARTIFICIAL INTELLIGENCE

In the exploratory voyage through the corridors of fractal mysticism, we now arrive at a juncture where the sacred geometries of the universe intertwine with the most profound creation of human intellect: artificial intelligence (AI). This chapter delves into the intricate relationship between fractal patterns, which are emblematic of the universe's inherent complexity, and AI, an emergent force that holds the potential to model, understand, and even reflect these cosmic principles.

Artificial Intelligence: Echoing the Fractal Cosmos

Artificial intelligence has burgeoned from rudimentary algorithms to sophisticated systems capable of mimicking human cognition. Interestingly, AI's developmental trajectory mirrors the fractal patterns it seeks to emulate: from simple rules emerge highly complex behaviors. Neural networks, the quintessential architecture of AI, exhibit a fractal-like structure. Layers of interconnected nodes (neurons) process information in a manner that could be seen as analogous to the recursive processes found in natural fractals.

AI and Fractal Generativity

One of the most compelling intersections of AI and fractal mysticism is in the realm of generative art. AI algorithms, particularly those employing deep learning techniques, have been trained to create fractal imagery that is not only visually stunning but also bears an uncanny resemblance to the archetypal patterns found in nature and sacred geometry. These images serve as a testament to the potential of AI to not only understand but also to create representations of the mystical patterns that permeate our universe.

Spiritual Reflections in the Mirror of AI

AI's capability to reflect the principles of fractal mysticism extends beyond mere visual representation. The very principles that underpin the functioning of AI, such as recursive self-improvement and pattern recognition, echo the mystical concepts of infinite recursion and the search for underlying cosmic patterns. In a sense, AI can be seen as a digital mirror reflecting the infinite complexity and recursive nature of the universe. This not only provides a novel perspective on spiritual principles but also offers a tangible model to explore and understand them.

As we traverse the nexus of fractals and artificial intelligence, we are confronted with a vista that is both awe-inspiring and humbling. AI, as a product of human ingenuity, has the potential to unravel the sacred patterns embedded in the cosmos, offering insights into the mystical geometry that binds the universe. This journey through the intersection of fractals and AI is not only an intellectual pursuit but also a spiritual odyssey, as we witness the unfolding of cosmic principles through the lens of human-created technology.

In conclusion, this chapter has journeyed through the intricate relationship between fractal patterns and artificial intelligence, exploring how AI reflects and has the potential to deepen our understanding of fractal mysticism. As we venture further into the realms of complexity and consciousness, the convergence of these domains promises to unravel new dimensions of knowledge and spiritual insight.

CHAPTER 32: PSYCHOACTIVE SUBSTANCES AND ALTERED STATES

The enigmatic domain of fractal mysticism intersects intriguingly with the altered states of consciousness induced by psychoactive substances. This chapter delves into the profound role that these substances play in perceiving fractal patterns and facilitating mystical experiences. From the intricate visions summoned by the intake of ayahuasca in the Amazonian spiritual ceremonies to the geometric hallucinations induced by lysergic acid diethylamide (LSD), the interplay between psychoactive substances and fractal perception has fascinated scholars, mystics, and psychonauts alike.

Psychoactive Substances: A Gateway to the Fractal Universe

Psychoactive substances, ranging from ancient plant concoctions to modern synthetic compounds, have the unique ability to alter consciousness and perception. These alterations often manifest in the form of fractal visions—complex, self-similar patterns that recur at different scales and seem to echo the very structure of the universe. The use of such substances in sacred rituals and shamanic practices across various cultures underscores their perceived ability to act as a conduit to a more profound, interconnected reality.

Under the influence of these substances, the mind's eye witnesses a kaleidoscopic array of patterns and shapes, many of which bear a striking resemblance to the fractals found in nature and in mathematical constructs like the Mandelbrot Set. These experiences are not merely visual; they can profoundly alter one's sense of self, time, and space, offering a glimpse into the boundless, recursive nature of the cosmos.

Neurofractality: The Brain's Dance with Geometry

Contemporary research into the effects of psychoactive substances has revealed fascinating insights into how the brain constructs reality. Neuroimaging studies have shown that under the influence of psychedelics, the brain's communication patterns become more fractal-like. This heightened connectivity and complexity mirror the recursive, self-similar patterns found in fractal geometry, suggesting that the brain may enter a 'neurofractal' state.

This state of neurofractality could be the underlying mechanism through which these substances facilitate mystical experiences and perceptions of interconnectedness. By disrupting the brain's default mode network—a system thought to be associated with self-referential thoughts and ego-identity—psychoactive substances open the floodgates to a less constrained, more holistically interconnected mode of thinking. In this state, the boundaries between self and other, subject and object, begin to dissolve, and the fractal nature of reality becomes experientially evident.

The Ritualistic Context: Setting and Integration

While the pharmacological properties of psychoactive

substances play a significant role in shaping the fractal experience, the context in which they are consumed is equally important. Traditional cultures have long understood that the setting—encompassing the physical environment, the mental state of the participant, and the intentions behind the consumption—significantly influences the nature of the psychedelic journey.

In many shamanic traditions, psychoactive substances are consumed within a structured ritualistic framework, often guided by an experienced shaman who helps navigate the fractal landscapes of the mind. This ceremonial context serves to anchor the experience, imbuing it with a sense of sacredness and purpose. It also facilitates the integration of the fractal visions and insights into one's life, ensuring that the mystical revelations translate into lasting, transformative change.

Conclusion

The interplay between psychoactive substances and fractal perception offers a tantalizing glimpse into the nature of consciousness and the universe. As tools for exploring the fractal depths of the mind, these substances provide a unique lens through which to examine the mystical patterns that underpin reality. While their use is not without risks and necessitates careful consideration and respect, their potential to catalyze profound insights and spiritual awakenings cannot be understated. In the mosaic of fractal mysticism, psychoactive substances represent a potent piece, one that continues to captivate and illuminate the minds of those who venture into its intricate, recursive realms.

CHAPTER 33: COSMOLOGICAL PATTERNS AND COSMIC MYSTICISM

The grand tapestry of the cosmos is replete with patterns that transcend the bounds of human understanding, ensnaring the minds of both scientists and mystics alike. Chapter 33 delves into the mesmerizing realm of cosmological patterns, seeking to elucidate the spiritual meanings that lie interwoven within the fractal structures of the universe. As we embark on this exploration, we venture beyond the confines of terrestrial familiarity, setting our sights on the vast, star-strewn expanses that beckon with whispers of cosmic mysticism.

Fractal Cosmology: The Self-Similarity of the Universe

The concept of self-similarity, a cornerstone of fractal geometry, finds a profound echo in the cosmos. It suggests that the structural motifs we observe in the microcosmic scale reverberate across the celestial canvas, manifesting in the clustering of galaxies, the intricate filaments of cosmic webs, and the enigmatic patterns of nebulae. These cosmic structures hint at an underlying fractal nature, implying that the universe might indeed be a fractal entity, embodying self-similarity across unfathomable scales. This realization posits a universe where the part reflects the whole, a concept deeply resonant with spiritual philosophies that see the individual as a microcosm of the divine macrocosm.

Cosmic Background Radiation: Echoes of the Primordial

The Cosmic Microwave Background (CMB) radiation, a relic of the universe's fiery infancy, serves as a celestial canvas for the earliest imprints of fractal patterns. Fluctuations in the CMB provide us with a cryptic map, an embryonic snapshot that contains the seeds of future cosmic structures. The enigmatic cold and hot spots observed in the CMB signal the genesis of galactic clusters and voids, akin to a cosmic mandala that holds the secrets of the universe's inception. The spiritual parallel here is uncanny, mirroring the mystic's pursuit of primordial wisdom, the quest for the original Word or Sound from which creation sprang forth.

Quantum Entanglement: A Fractal Web of Connectedness

Quantum entanglement, one of the most bewildering phenomena in physics, suggests that particles can become linked in such a way that the state of one instantaneously affects the state of another, regardless of the distance separating them. This non-local connection paints a picture of a universe where separateness is an illusion, and all is interwoven in a complex, fractal web. Mystical traditions have long held the belief in an interconnected universe, where every atom is a part of a divine whole, echoing the hermetic adage, "As above, so below, as within, so without, as the universe, so the soul."

Dark Matter and Dark Energy: The Unseen Fractal Scaffold

The enigmatic dark matter and dark energy, which together comprise the lion's share of the universe's mass-energy content, remain largely elusive. Yet, their gravitational influence molds the cosmic structures, acting as an invisible fractal scaffold that shapes the observable universe. This dark sector of the cosmos parallels the mystical notion of the unseen, the transcendent reality that shapes and underpins the manifest world, a hidden tapestry that weaves the fabric of the cosmos into coherent form.

Cosmological Constant: The Rhythm of the Cosmic Dance

The cosmological constant, a term in Einstein's equations of general relativity, points to a mysterious anti-gravity force that pervades the vacuum of space, driving the universe's accelerated expansion. This expansion, a sort of cosmic dance, is replete with rhythm and pattern, echoing the fractal nature of existence. Mystics perceive the universe as a grand dance of Shiva or the symphony of the spheres, a cosmic ballet choreographed by the divine, with each celestial entity moving in perfect harmony, according to sacred, geometric patterns.

In exploring the fractal structures of the cosmos and their spiritual connotations, Chapter 33 ventures into territories where science and mysticism converge, each offering a lens to glimpse the ineffable beauty of the universe. Through the fractal lens, the cosmos emerges not merely as an assemblage of stars and galaxies, but as a sacred geometry, a cosmic mandala that dances to the rhythm of the divine. Herein lies the allure of cosmic mysticism, where the pursuit of scientific understanding becomes an act of spiritual reverence, and the study of the universe becomes a path to transcendence.

CHAPTER 34: QUANTUM COMPUTING AND MYSTICAL COMPLEXITY

Quantum computing and mystical complexity are two domains that, at first glance, appear to be worlds apart. The former is rooted in the empirical and precise world of science, while the latter is often associated with the esoteric and intangible realms of spirituality. Yet, as our understanding of the universe becomes increasingly sophisticated, it is becoming clear that these two spheres are not just interconnected; they may in fact be intricately woven into the same fabric of reality. This chapter delves into the fascinating nexus between quantum computing and mystical complexity, exploring how these seemingly disparate fields are converging in ways that could profoundly transform our understanding of the cosmos and our place within it.

Quantum Computing: Unleashing New Realities

Quantum computing represents a radical departure from classical computing. While classical computers operate on bits that can be either 0 or 1, quantum computers use quantum bits, or qubits, which can exist in multiple states simultaneously thanks to the principle of superposition. This feature, along with entanglement, allows quantum computers to process and store an exponentially greater amount of information compared to their classical counterparts, providing the potential to solve problems that are currently intractable.

But quantum computing is more than just a tool for enhanced computational power. It's a gateway to understanding and manipulating the very fabric of reality. The principles that govern quantum computing are derived from the same principles that underlie the universe at its most fundamental level. In doing so, quantum computers serve as a bridge between the abstract, mathematical realm of quantum mechanics and the tangible reality we experience.

The Interplay with Mystical Complexity

Mysticism has long grappled with the notion of complexity, often meditating on the idea that simple universal truths can give rise to infinitely complex phenomena. Mystical traditions across the world have contemplated the intricate patterns found in nature and human consciousness, seeking to understand the underlying order amidst apparent chaos.

Quantum computing offers a new lens through which to view these ancient ideas. The way in which qubits interact and give rise to complex computational results mirrors the mystical belief in simple laws giving birth to a multiplicity of forms and experiences. The interplay between the two, the computational and the mystical, creates a rich tapestry that we are only just beginning to explore.

Modeling Spiritual Systems

One of the most intriguing applications of quantum computing in the realm of mysticism is the potential to model complex spiritual systems. Just as quantum computers are being used to simulate complex molecular structures and predict weather patterns, they could also be employed to model systems that are central to mystical thought, such as the interconnectivity of consciousness or the patterns of synchronicity that many believe govern the universe.

These models could offer insights into age-old spiritual questions, providing a new framework for understanding concepts like fate, destiny, and the interplay between free will and determinism. They could also help bridge the gap between the empirical and the spiritual, grounding mystical beliefs in a computational framework that is both rigorous and expansive.

Quantum Entanglement and Mystical Unity

Quantum entanglement, a phenomenon where particles become intertwined in such a way that the state of one instantaneously influences the state of another, regardless of distance, resonates deeply with mystical notions of oneness and interconnectedness. Many spiritual traditions speak of the fundamental unity of all things, a concept that quantum entanglement seems to echo.

This parallel opens up profound philosophical and spiritual questions. If the universe is indeed entangled at a quantum level, what does this mean for our understanding of separation and individuality? How does this inform mystical experiences of unity and transcendence? Quantum computing not only brings these questions to the forefront but also offers a framework for exploring them in concrete terms.

Challenges and Ethical Considerations

While the potential of quantum computing to model mystical complexity is vast, it also raises significant challenges and ethical considerations. The power of quantum computing, like any technology, can be used for both constructive and destructive ends. Furthermore, there are questions about the reductionism inherent in trying to model spiritual experiences, which are deeply personal and often transcend rational explanation.

It is crucial, therefore, to approach this convergence of quantum computing and mystical complexity with both enthusiasm and caution, ensuring that these tools are used to enhance our understanding and appreciation of the mystical, rather than to diminish or exploit it.

In conclusion, Chapter 34 explores the intricate and profound connections between quantum computing and mystical complexity. As we continue to expand our understanding of both, we are discovering that the universe is even more interconnected and wondrous than we could have imagined. This convergence offers a new path for exploring age-old spiritual questions, bringing us closer to unraveling the sacred patterns that weave the fabric of the cosmos.

CHAPTER 35: THE ETHICS OF MYSTICAL GEOMETRY

In this intricate lattice of ideas we've constructed, spanning from the rudimentary understanding of fractals to their most elaborate applications in mysticism, we've reached a juncture that demands a pivot from the descriptive to the normative. Chapter 35 wades into the rich but often turbulent waters of ethics, specifically examining the moral implications of applying fractal mysticism in various domains of human experience. As we delve into this labyrinth, we confront questions not just about what is or can be, but about what ought to be.

Ethical Frameworks and Fractal Mysticism

To navigate the ethical dimension of fractal mysticism, we must first anchor ourselves in ethical theory. Traditional frameworks like deontology, consequentialism, and virtue ethics provide lenses through which to scrutinize the moral underpinnings of fractal mysticism. These paradigms compel us to ask poignant questions: Does the application of fractal mysticism respect the intrinsic dignity of individuals (a deontological perspective)? Do the outcomes of applying fractal patterns in social or individual spheres optimize well-being or happiness (a consequentialist approach)? Or does engaging with fractal mysticism cultivate virtues and a sense of fulfillment in practitioners (a virtue ethics perspective)?

Responsibility in Dissemination

With fractal mysticism intersecting numerous disciplines, from architecture to cognitive science, the responsibility of accurately representing and disseminating fractal principles becomes paramount. Misinformation or superficial understanding could lead to misapplications with ethically problematic consequences. This responsibility extends to educators, authors, practitioners, and even lay enthusiasts, all of whom contribute to the collective consciousness surrounding fractals.

Technological and Environmental Considerations

In the realm of technology, fractal algorithms underpin advancements in signal processing, computer graphics, and even artificial intelligence. Yet, with great power comes great responsibility. The ethical use of fractals in technology demands consideration of privacy, autonomy, and the potential exacerbation of social inequities. Environmentally, fractal patterns appear ubiquitously in nature, and our actions that affect the environment—whether through urban planning, deforestation, or climate change—can disrupt these patterns. A deeper understanding of fractal mysticism instills a reverence for these natural patterns and a moral imperative to preserve them.

Spirituality and Ethics

At its core, fractal mysticism is a spiritual endeavor. It seeks not only to explain but to connect, suggesting an intrinsic harmony between the cosmos and the self. Yet spirituality is not ethically neutral. Practitioners of fractal mysticism must be wary of cultural appropriation, respecting the origins and sacredness of the patterns they employ. Furthermore, spiritual guidance, when framed through the lens of fractal mysticism, must be offered with compassion and ethical integrity, ensuring it empowers rather than manipulates or exploits.

The Ethics of Interpretation

Fractal mysticism is inherently interpretative, finding meaning and significance in patterns that might appear chaotic or random to the uninitiated. This interpretative act is not just an intellectual exercise; it's a moral one. How one interprets a fractal pattern can have implications for how one views the universe, their place in it, and their treatment of others. The ethical implications of interpretation demand a level of intellectual humility and openness, acknowledging the limits of our understanding and the potential for multiple, equally valid interpretations.

In sum, the ethics of fractal mysticism weave through every aspect of its application, from the dissemination of knowledge to the environmental and technological implications, and the spiritual and interpretative dimensions. As we delve deeper into this domain, it becomes increasingly apparent that fractal mysticism is not just a passive reflection of the cosmos but an active engagement with the moral fabric of our reality. It challenges us to not only uncover patterns in the chaos but also to consider the ethical patterns of our actions as we navigate the intricate web of existence.

CHAPTER 36: MULTIVERSE THEORIES AND ETERNAL RETURN

As we delve deeper into the realms of complexity, our journey brings us to the forefront of cosmological speculation and the fascinating interplay between fractal geometry and multiverse theories. The notion of multiple universes, each with its own unique tapestry of cosmic events, has tantalized both scientists and spiritual seekers alike. This chapter explores the intriguing parallels between multiverse concepts and the mystical doctrine of eternal return, all through the intricate lens of fractal mysticism.

The Multiverse Tapestry

The multiverse theory posits that our universe might be just one of an unfathomable number of universes, each existing independently with its own set of physical laws and constants. This cosmic quilt is a tantalizing thought experiment that has its roots in various scientific theories, ranging from quantum mechanics to string theory. At its core, the multiverse can be envisioned as a fractal structure, where each universe represents a unique iteration, stemming from a set of initial conditions and unfolding in an infinite variety of ways.

Eternal Return and Fractal Iterations

The doctrine of eternal return, a philosophical and spiritual concept, suggests that the universe and all events within it are destined to recur in a self-similar form an infinite number of times. This cyclical view of time and existence bears a striking resemblance to the recursive nature of fractals. In both concepts, the notion of infinity plays a central role – the endless repetition of patterns in fractals mirrors the eternal recurrence of cosmic events. The self-similarity of fractals provides a compelling geometric analogy to the cycles of time and existence posited by the doctrine of eternal return.

Fractal Geometry in Multiverse Theories

Fractal geometry offers a powerful framework for visualizing the structure of the multiverse. In a fractal multiverse, each universe can be considered a fractal iteration, branching off from a common origin much like the repeating patterns in a Mandelbrot set. The intricate, self-similar structures seen in fractals provide a captivating model for the potentially infinite variety of universes, each with its own set of physical laws, constants, and cosmic events.

Moreover, the boundary conditions of one universe could serve as the genesis for another, just as the border of a fractal pattern holds the seed for further complexity. This recursive process might continue ad infinitum, suggesting a fractal-like proliferation of universes across the cosmic fabric.

Implications for Mystical Thought

The marriage of multiverse theories and fractal geometry has profound implications for mystical thought. If we consider each universe as a unique expression of the divine, then the multiverse becomes a grand fractal manifestation of the sacred. The infinite diversity and complexity of the universes reflect the boundless nature of the divine, with each fractal iteration representing a distinct facet of the cosmic whole.

The doctrine of eternal return gains a new dimension when viewed through the prism of fractal multiverses. The endless cycles of existence take on a fractal quality, with each recurrence adding to the infinite complexity of the cosmic pattern. This perspective imbues the mystical journey with a sense of awe and wonder, as the seeker contemplates the unfathomable depth and intricacy of the divine fractal.

Conclusion

Chapter 36 has taken us on a voyage through the vast expanses of cosmic possibility, where the ideas of multiverses and eternal return intertwine with the mesmerizing patterns of fractal geometry. This exploration has not only expanded our understanding of the universe but also deepened our appreciation for the mystical dimensions of existence. As we stand at the crossroads of science and spirituality, the fractal tapestry of the multiverse serves as a profound reminder of the intricate beauty and eternal mystery that pervade the cosmos.

CHAPTER 37: THE UNCERTAINTY PRINCIPLE AND DIVINE MYSTERY

As we delve into the more advanced realms of fractal mysticism, the intersection of quantum mechanics and spiritual mysteries presents an enigmatic yet enthralling landscape. Central to this intersection is Heisenberg's Uncertainty Principle, a pillar of quantum mechanics, which states that the position and momentum of a particle cannot both be precisely known at the same time. This fundamental tenet of the quantum world paradoxically intertwines with the fabric of mystical experiences, where the divine often manifests in ambiguities and enigmas.

Quantum Mysticism: The Veil of Uncertainty

At the heart of quantum mysticism lies the notion that uncertainty is not merely a scientific concept but a fundamental aspect of the divine. Just as the Uncertainty Principle implies that there is a limit to what can be known about a particle's position and momentum, mystical traditions across cultures have long suggested that the divine essence cannot be fully comprehended or articulated by human intellect. This parallel draws an intriguing connection between the unpredictability of quantum particles and the ineffable nature of spiritual experiences.

In many mystical traditions, the divine is seen as an omnipresent force that transcends the boundaries of human understanding. The Uncertainty Principle metaphorically mirrors this by highlighting the limitations of our knowledge and the inherent unpredictability of the quantum realm. It compels us to embrace the unknown, a sentiment echoed in various mystical teachings that encourage an acceptance of mystery as a pathway to spiritual enlightenment.

Fractals: Patterns of Uncertainty

The Uncertainty Principle's implications extend beyond the realm of particles and into the intricate world of fractals. Fractals are patterns that repeat at different scales, often exhibiting complex and unpredictable behavior. This chaotic yet ordered nature is reminiscent of the quantum world's inherent uncertainty. Just as it is impossible to predict the exact location and momentum of a quantum particle, fractals too can be unpredictable, their patterns emerging and dissipating in seemingly random ways.

However, within this randomness lies a deeper order, a hidden symmetry that resonates with the mystical belief in an underlying unity within the cosmos. The fractal, with its infinite complexity, becomes a symbol for the divine, a manifestation of the sacred that both conceals and reveals. It teaches us that within uncertainty and chaos, there is a cosmic order, a spiritual geometry that guides the universe.

Embracing Mystery: A Path to Spiritual Awakening

The Uncertainty Principle not only challenges our

understanding of the physical world but also invites us to reassess our approach to spiritual truths. It encourages a humble acceptance of the limits of human knowledge and an openness to the mysteries of existence. In many spiritual traditions, this embracing of mystery is seen as a crucial step towards enlightenment.

Mysticism often emphasizes the importance of personal experience and intuition over intellectual understanding. In this light, the Uncertainty Principle can be viewed as a metaphor for the mystical journey. Just as a quantum particle's behavior eludes definitive prediction, the divine eludes definitive description. The mystic's path, therefore, is one of exploration and discovery, guided by an acceptance of uncertainty and a reverence for the unknown.

Conclusion

Heisenberg's Uncertainty Principle, a cornerstone of quantum mechanics, reveals profound connections to the enigmatic realms of fractal mysticism. It echoes the ancient wisdom that the divine essence is shrouded in mystery, and that uncertainty is not a hindrance but a gateway to deeper spiritual insights. As we traverse the complex landscape of fractals, quantum mechanics, and mysticism, we find that uncertainty is not just a scientific truth but a sacred principle that invites us to explore the divine mysteries with wonder and humility.

CHAPTER 38: THE FOURTH DIMENSION AND SPIRITUAL ASCENSION

In our continual quest to decipher the enigmas of the universe, we venture beyond the tangible dimensions of our perceivable reality into the abstract realms that transcend ordinary experiences. Chapter 38 invites us to explore the concept of the fourth dimension and its profound implications on spiritual ascension, a complex and advanced facet of fractal mysticism.

Unfolding the Fourth Dimension

The concept of dimensions extends beyond the familiar three-dimensional space encompassing length, width, and height. The fourth dimension, often referred to in the realms of theoretical physics and mathematics, adds a new layer of complexity to our understanding of the universe. It's a dimension not of space, but of time – or more abstractly, a dimension that integrates with the spatial dimensions to form a higher-order fabric of reality.

In spiritual discourses, the fourth dimension is perceived as a plane of existence that transcends the physical confines of the three-dimensional world. It's often associated with higher states of consciousness, timelessness, and the realm where the spiritual becomes tangible. The transition from three-dimensional space into the fourth dimension is metaphorically akin to spiritual ascension – a shift from a limited, material-focused existence to a higher, more spiritually aligned state of being.

Geometrical Portals to Ascension

Fractal geometry serves as a mathematical bridge to understanding higher dimensions. Fractals, with their self-similar patterns repeating infinitely at different scales, provide a conceptual framework for visualizing the complex structures of higher-dimensional spaces. In the context of the fourth dimension, fractals can be seen as geometrical portals or maps that guide the consciousness through the intricate landscapes of higher-dimensional realms.

The Mandelbrot set, a well-known fractal, is a striking example. Its boundary is infinitely complex, and as one zooms in, similar patterns emerge ad infinitum, suggesting the endless depth and complexity that higher dimensions encapsulate. This fractal characteristic resonates with the spiritual journey of ascension, where one continually delves deeper into the layers of consciousness, each layer revealing profound truths and greater complexities.

Spiritual Ascension and Higher-Dimensional Spaces

In many spiritual traditions, the journey of ascension is described as a path of increasing vibration, moving from lower, denser states to higher, more refined levels of energy and consciousness. This journey is not just metaphorical but can be interpreted through the lens of higher-dimensional spaces. As one ascends spiritually, they move closer to the fourth dimension, where time and space converge, and the limitations of the physical world dissolve.

This convergence of time and space in the fourth dimension aligns with the notion of oneness that many mystical traditions uphold. In this higher-dimensional space, the past, present, and future coalesce, providing a state of eternal now, a moment where all points in time become accessible. It's a realm where the illusion of separation fades, and the interconnectedness of all things becomes the prevailing truth.

Implications for Fractal Mysticism

The exploration of the fourth dimension and its relationship with spiritual ascension enriches the narrative of fractal mysticism. It underscores the idea that the universe's complexity is not just inherent in its physical structures but also woven into the fabric of its spiritual dimensions. The fourth dimension, as a higher order of existence, offers a paradigm through which we can understand the interconnectedness of all things, the cyclical nature of time, and the transcendent qualities of consciousness.

Fractal mysticism, in this light, is not merely an intellectual exercise but a transformative journey. It invites us to expand our perception, to embrace the complexity of the cosmos, and to ascend toward a higher state of spiritual awareness. The fourth dimension, with its profound implications, serves as a reminder that our reality is but a shadow of a more intricate, multidimensional universe, waiting to be explored and understood.

In conclusion, Chapter 38 illuminates the concept of the fourth dimension and its significance in the tapestry of fractal mysticism. It serves as a profound reflection on the nature of spiritual ascension, the complexities of higher-dimensional spaces, and the infinite depths of consciousness that fractal geometry helps us to navigate. As we contemplate the mysteries of the fourth dimension, we are reminded of the boundless potential for spiritual growth and the vast expanse of the universe that awaits our exploration.

CHAPTER 39: GÖDEL'S INCOMPLETENESS THEOREMS AND SPIRITUAL LIMITATIONS

In the labyrinthine corridors of mathematics and spirituality, there exist parallels that mystify the rational mind and ignite the spirit of inquiry. Chapter 39 of "Fractal Mysticism: Sacred Patterns in the Universe" embarks on an intellectual odyssey to explore one such parallel: the curious intersections between Gödel's Incompleteness Theorems and the perceived limitations in spiritual understanding.

The Incompleteness of Systems

Kurt Gödel, an Austrian logician, mathematician, and philosopher, presented the world with his Incompleteness Theorems in 1931, shaking the foundations of mathematics and logic. Gödel postulated that within any sufficiently complex axiomatic system, there are propositions that cannot be proved nor disproved based on the axioms within that system. In essence, no system could be both consistent and complete; there would always be truths that exist beyond the system's capability to prove.

This notion of inherent limitations within a system bears a remarkable resemblance to the mystic's view of the spiritual universe. Just as mathematics grapples with truths that elude proof within its system, mysticism acknowledges the existence of spiritual truths and realities that transcend human understanding or expression within the confines of physical reality and rational thought.

Paradoxes and Mysticism

The second part of Gödel's theorems introduces self-referential paradoxes, where a system may assert a statement that refers back to itself in a way that creates an unsolvable paradox. This self-reference is not foreign to the realm of mysticism. Many spiritual traditions revel in paradoxes as a way to illustrate the limitations of human logic and the vastness of the divine. Consider the Zen koan or the Sufi parable; both use paradox as a tool to jolt the seeker out of conventional patterns of thought, pushing them towards a deeper, more intuitive understanding.

The Limits of Language and Symbolism

Gödel's work also illuminates the inadequacies of language and symbolism in fully encapsulating complex truths. In mathematics, symbols and equations are the languages through which ideas are conveyed, yet Gödel showed that there are truths that these symbols cannot fully express or prove. Similarly, mysticism acknowledges that the divine, the spiritual, and the sacred are often ineffable, transcending the confines of language and symbols. Mystics have long posited that the ultimate truths of the universe are beyond verbal or symbolic articulation and must be experienced directly to be fully understood.

Implications for Fractal Mysticism

Fractal mysticism, the central theme of this tome, is not immune to the implications of Gödel's theorems. The fractal nature of the universe, with its infinitely recurring patterns, suggests a complex system – one that may also be subject to the limitations Gödel described. It invites speculation: Are there aspects of the fractal universe that are inherently unknowable? Do the patterns we observe in nature hint at a larger, incomprehensible truth, just as mathematical theorems may hint at unprovable truths?

Embracing the Unknown

The real beauty of Gödel's theorems, when applied metaphorically to spiritual exploration, is not in the limitations they impose, but in the humility and wonder they instill. They remind us that in both mathematics and mysticism, there is always a frontier beyond which lies the unknown, the unexplored, and perhaps the unexplorable. This is not a cause for frustration, but rather a call to embrace the mystery, to revel in the awe of the infinite, and to accept that some truths may reside in the realm of the experiential rather than the explainable.

In conclusion, Gödel's Incompleteness Theorems serve as a profound metaphor in the study of fractal mysticism. They highlight the parallels between the limitations of mathematical systems and the ineffable nature of spiritual truths. As seekers of knowledge, whether through the lens of science, mathematics, or spirituality, embracing the unknown is not an admission of defeat but a testament to the boundless curiosity that defines the human spirit. In this light, Gödel's theorems are not merely mathematical constructs; they are beacons that illuminate the path of inquiry and introspection, guiding us through the sacred patterns of the universe.

CHAPTER 40: NEURAL NETWORKS AND THE MIND'S FRACTALS

The human mind is an enigmatic tapestry interwoven with patterns that echo the fractal geometry pervading the cosmos. This chapter delves into the fascinating parallels between neural networks — the intricate web of neurons in the human brain — and the fractals that represent the universe's inherent complexity. We explore how our cerebral architecture may be utilizing fractal-like processes for cognition and spirituality, shedding light on the profound intersection of the physical and the metaphysical.

Cerebral Fractals: Mind as a Mirror of the Cosmos

The brain, with its approximately 86 billion neurons, operates through an intricate network of connections and signals. These neural networks, like the fractal patterns observed in nature, exhibit a complexity that seems to transcend the sum of their parts. Just as a fractal's pattern repeats across different scales, the structure and functionality of the brain also showcase a fractal nature. Dendritic trees — the branching extensions of neurons — and the brain's vascular system both display self-similar patterns that are hallmarks of fractal geometry.

These fractal attributes are not merely structural; they extend to the dynamic processes of the brain. The firing patterns of neurons, the unfolding of thoughts, and even the trajectory of consciousness itself reveal fractal characteristics. They echo the iterative process of fractals, where simple rules applied repeatedly can generate profound complexity. This resonates with the brain's capacity to learn and adapt, transforming simple neural impulses into the intricate tapestry of human experience.

The Spirituality of Neural Fractals

The concept of fractal mysticism isn't merely an abstract, mathematical curiosity; it finds a profound echo in the human experience. Our spiritual encounters, those moments when we touch the numinous or transcend the ordinary, are often accompanied by a sense of boundless complexity and infinite depth. It's intriguing to consider whether our spiritual experiences are facilitated by the fractal nature of our neural networks.

Meditative states, moments of epiphany, and even the phenomenon of déjà vu could be manifestations of the brain's fractal processes. These experiences often involve a recursive deepening into the self or the cosmos, a journey that mirrors the never-ending paths of fractals. By understanding the fractal nature of our minds, we might gain insights into the spiritual practices that have evolved across cultures, designed, perhaps instinctively, to resonate with these patterns.

Cognitive Fractals and the Evolution of Consciousness

The fractal-like nature of our neural networks isn't just a static property; it may be a driving force in the evolution of consciousness itself. The iterative learning processes of the brain, its capacity for pattern recognition, and the recursive deepening of understanding all suggest that our consciousness might be a product of fractal computation.

The development of consciousness, from its primordial roots to its current complexity, may parallel the iterative processes seen in fractal geometry. Just as fractals become more intricate with each iteration, our consciousness might be evolving into greater complexity through recursive cycles of learning and adaptation.

Summary

In this chapter, we've embarked on a cerebral odyssey, exploring the fractal nature of the human mind and its implications for cognition and spirituality. We've seen how the brain's structure and processes echo the patterns of the cosmos, and we've pondered the spiritual significance of these parallels. By understanding the fractal geometry inherent in our neural networks, we might gain deeper insights into the nature of consciousness, the evolution of our cognitive capacities, and the spiritual experiences that have fascinated humanity since time immemorial. This exploration blurs the lines between the physical and the metaphysical, hinting at a fractal tapestry that interweaves the universe, the mind, and the soul.

CHAPTER 41: VIRTUAL REALITY AND SIMULATED SPIRITUALITY

The realm of virtual reality (VR) has expanded beyond mere entertainment, morphing into a conduit for spiritual exploration and awakening. This chapter delves into the interplay between virtual realities and spiritual experiences, examining how simulated environments can serve as a medium for mystical insights and practices.

The Nexus Between Virtual Realities and Mystical Experiences

Virtual reality, by its very definition, creates an artificial world, an immersive simulation that can engage multiple senses. The most compelling aspect of VR is its ability to transport the user into alternate realities, bending the laws of physics and defying the constraints of the material world. It is in this space where the mystical and the virtual converge, offering a fertile ground for spiritual exploration.

Consider the fractal nature of reality, a concept deeply rooted in both science and spirituality. Fractals are infinitely complex patterns that are self-similar across different scales, a characteristic manifested in natural phenomena as well as in the mathematical constructs of the Mandelbrot set. In VR, these fractal patterns can be rendered with hyper-realistic detail, allowing users to navigate and interact with them in ways that are impossible in the physical world. This immersive exploration can evoke a profound sense of interconnectedness and infinity, hallmarks of mystical experiences.

Furthermore, VR enables the creation of sacred spaces and temples, meticulously designed with sacred geometry and fractal architecture, thus facilitating meditative and contemplative experiences. Users can enter these virtual sanctuaries to engage in spiritual practices or simply to seek solace and introspection, untethered from the distractions and limitations of the tangible world.

Simulated Spirituality: A New Frontier or a Digital Illusion?

As we delve deeper into the possibilities of VR in the spiritual realm, it's essential to address a critical question: does simulated spirituality hold the same value as traditional spiritual experiences? Some argue that virtual spiritual experiences are mere illusions, lacking the authenticity and depth of real-world practices. However, others posit that the essence of spirituality transcends the medium through which it is experienced. After all, if the mystical journey is about transcending the physical and reaching into the metaphysical, then does the medium truly matter?

Virtual reality can serve as a powerful tool for visualizing and embodying complex spiritual concepts. For instance, VR can simulate the experience of traversing higher-dimensional spaces, offering a visceral understanding of theories that remain abstract and elusive in the physical world. This can lead to profound epiphanies and a deeper comprehension of the mystical aspects of existence.

Moreover, VR can democratize spiritual experiences, making

them accessible to individuals who may not have the means or ability to travel to sacred sites or partake in traditional rituals. In a way, it can break down barriers and open the doors to inclusive and universal spiritual exploration.

The Potential Pitfalls of Virtual Spirituality

While the benefits of integrating VR into spiritual practices are manifold, it is crucial to remain cognizant of the potential pitfalls. One major concern is the possibility of escapism, where individuals may prefer the simulated spiritual experiences over engaging with the real world. This could lead to a detachment from reality and a reluctance to confront the tangible challenges of life.

Another issue pertains to the commercialization of spiritual experiences. As VR technology becomes more prevalent, there is a risk of sacred practices being commodified, stripped of their profundity, and sold as mere entertainment. This could dilute the essence of spirituality, reducing it to a product rather than a profound journey of self-discovery.

In conclusion, virtual reality presents a paradoxical yet intriguing frontier in the realm of spirituality. It holds the promise of deepening our understanding of mystical concepts and making spiritual experiences more accessible. Yet, it also poses challenges and raises questions about the nature of authenticity and the potential for misuse. As we navigate this digital terrain, it is imperative to approach it with discernment, wisdom, and a commitment to preserving the sanctity of the spiritual quest.

CHAPTER 42: FRACTAL ECONOMICS AND SPIRITUAL WEALTH

In the tapestry of fractal mysticism, the interplay between chaos and order does not confine itself to mere geometric abstractions or cosmological ruminations; it seeps into the very fabric of our daily lives, influencing the structures of our economies and the philosophies of our wealth. This chapter aims to unravel the enigmatic patterns that fractal economics weave, expounding upon how these patterns parallel with spiritual wealth and fractal mysticism.

Fractal Economics: The New Paradigm

Economics, traditionally seen through the lens of linear models and equilibrium theories, has undergone a paradigmatic shift with the advent of fractal analysis. This paradigm posits that economies are not predictable, linear systems tending towards equilibrium but are instead complex, dynamic, and inherently chaotic structures. They exhibit self-similarity and scale invariance, hallmark traits of fractals.

Stock market fluctuations, consumer behavior patterns, and even large-scale economic cycles can be observed through the fractal lens. For instance, the erratic ups and downs of the stock market, when plotted over time, reveal a fractal nature.

This means that patterns of behavior on a small scale (daily fluctuations) can be fractal echoes of larger-scale patterns (market cycles over decades). These insights have profound implications for how economists predict market behaviors and how investors navigate the treacherous waters of finance.

Spiritual Wealth: Abundance in Complexity

In the realms of fractal mysticism, wealth transcends the material. Spiritual wealth, a term steeped in the intangible and infinite, is akin to the fractal patterns that stretch endlessly into the cosmos. It is about richness of the soul, abundance of inner peace, and the treasure trove of wisdom. Just as fractals can be infinitely complex yet arise from simple rules, spiritual wealth can be seen as a profound inner complexity arising from simple spiritual principles such as compassion, mindfulness, and gratitude.

In the spiritual context, wealth is not a static entity to be accumulated but a dynamic, flowing state of being. It is the ability to resonate with the universe's frequency, to be in harmony with its chaotic yet ordered dance. It involves recognizing the interconnectedness of all things and finding abundance in the relationships and experiences that shape our existence.

Intersecting Pathways: Fractals in Economy and Spirituality

The intersection of fractal economics and spiritual wealth is where the material meets the mystical. It lies in understanding that the unpredictability and complexity of economic systems are not hurdles to be overcome but realities to be embraced, much like the chaotic yet harmonious nature of the universe.

One tangible manifestation of this intersection is the concept of 'circular economy', a model that mirrors the recursive nature of fractals. In a circular economy, resources are reused, repurposed, and recycled in a continuous loop, mimicking the self-sustaining patterns found in nature's fractals. This model is not only economically sound but also resonates deeply with the principles of spiritual wealth, emphasizing sustainability, interconnectedness, and balance.

Another example is the rise of social and impact investing, where the measure of wealth is not just financial returns but also the positive impact on society and the environment. Investors are increasingly recognizing that true wealth is about creating value that resonates with the fractal patterns of social and ecological harmony.

Challenges and Considerations

While the principles of fractal economics and the pursuit of spiritual wealth offer a hopeful vision of the future, their implementation is not without challenges. The complexity of economic systems and the deeply ingrained habits of materialistic wealth accumulation make the shift towards a fractal-based economic model a daunting task. Moreover, the subjective nature of spiritual wealth makes its integration into economic models an intricate endeavor.

Nevertheless, as our understanding of fractals and their applications deepens, so too does our ability to navigate these complexities. The fusion of fractal economics with spiritual wealth is not a straightforward path but a winding journey through the intricate landscapes of chaos and order, materiality and mysticism.

In summary, Chapter 42 weaves a complex narrative that bridges the material with the mystical, exploring how fractal economics and spiritual wealth intertwine in a dance of chaos and order. It challenges traditional notions of wealth and economic structures, offering a vision of a world where material abundance and spiritual richness coexist in harmony, resonating with the sacred patterns that pervade the universe.

CHAPTER 43: CYBERNETICS AND THE FEEDBACK LOOP OF SPIRITUALITY

In the labyrinthine corridors of human understanding, cybernetics emerges as a compass, guiding us through the complexities of systems, feedback, and self-regulation. The term, originating from the Greek "kybernētēs", meaning "steersman" or "governor", was repurposed in the 20th century to denote the study of control and communication in the animal and the machine. This chapter delves into the fascinating interplay between cybernetic principles and spirituality, unraveling the profound symbiosis between feedback loops and spiritual evolution.

The Cybernetic Framework

At the heart of cybernetics lies the concept of the feedback loop, a system's mechanism for self-regulation through constant monitoring and adjustment based on the discrepancies between the actual and desired states. This process is ubiquitous, governing everything from the homeostasis in biological organisms to the function of a thermostat maintaining room temperature. In the context of spirituality, feedback loops manifest in the form of introspection, meditation, and other reflective practices where the individual assesses their spiritual state, identifies deviations from their desired path, and enacts changes to align with their higher purpose.

Feedback Loops in Spiritual Practices

Spiritual traditions across the globe have intuitively harnessed the power of feedback loops. In Buddhism, the concept of mindfulness embodies a feedback mechanism where one continually observes their thoughts and sensations without judgment, gently steering them towards equanimity. The mystical practices of Sufism involve a similar process of self-observation and refinement through zikr (remembrance of God), enabling practitioners to navigate closer to the Divine essence. These practices, though diverse in form, share a cybernetic skeleton — the relentless pursuit of spiritual equilibrium through recursive self-assessment and adaptation.

The Recursive Nature of Spiritual Growth

Cybernetics and spirituality converge on the principle of recursion — the process of repeating items in a self-similar way. Spiritual growth is inherently recursive; it is a journey of returning to core values and truths, revisiting and reinterpreting them at higher planes of understanding. This spiral progression, akin to ascending a fractal staircase, epitomizes the recursive essence of cybernetics, where systems continuously cycle through feedback loops, each iteration propelling them closer to optimization. The spiritual aspirant, likewise, evolves through recursive introspection, each cycle imbuing them with deeper insights and greater alignment with their spiritual ideals.

The Symbiotic Dance of Chaos and Order

Cybernetics illuminates the delicate dance between chaos and order, a theme resonant in fractal mysticism. Chaos, often perceived as disorder, is integral to the emergence of new patterns and complexities in systems. Similarly, spirituality recognizes that periods of chaos and uncertainty are catalysts for transformation and growth. Order, on the other hand, provides structure and predictability, enabling the assimilation of chaotic insights into coherent spiritual wisdom. Cybernetic systems thrive at the edge of chaos and order, in a dynamic equilibrium that fosters continuous evolution — a state mirrored in the spiritual pursuit of harmony between earthly experiences and transcendent truths.

Technological Interfaces of Spirituality

In an age where technology permeates every facet of life, cybernetics offers a lens to explore the spiritual potential of technological interfaces. Biofeedback devices, for instance, provide real-time data on physiological functions, enabling individuals to consciously regulate stress and enhance mindfulness — a cybernetic feedback loop applied to spiritual well-being. Virtual reality environments can simulate sacred spaces, facilitating immersive spiritual experiences that transcend physical boundaries. These technological embodiments of cybernetic principles herald a new paradigm, where spirituality and technology coalesce, each enriching the other through reciprocal feedback loops.

Conclusion

The exploration of cybernetics in the context of spirituality reveals a profound resonance between these seemingly disparate domains. Feedback loops, the cornerstone of cybernetic systems, are deeply entrenched in spiritual practices, enabling individuals to navigate the intricacies of their inner landscapes. The recursive nature of spiritual growth mirrors the iterative processes fundamental to cybernetic systems, highlighting a shared architecture of evolution. As we stand at the confluence of spirituality and technology, cybernetics offers a transformative framework, guiding us towards a harmonious integration of these realms and unveiling the boundless potential of their synergy.

CHAPTER 44: CHAOS MAGICK AND CONTEMPORARY PRACTICES

In the contemporary tapestry of spiritual practices, Chaos Magick emerges as a particularly intriguing thread, intertwining the ancient with the avant-garde. This chapter delves into the enigmatic realm of Chaos Magick, a paradigm that embraces the unpredictable and nonlinear nature of reality, resonating deeply with the principles of fractal mysticism discussed in previous chapters.

The Essence of Chaos Magick

Chaos Magick, born out of the countercultural tumult of the 1970s, represents a radical departure from traditional ceremonial magick. It is predicated on the belief that belief itself is a tool; practitioners, known as chaotes, often adopt and discard diverse beliefs and deities not as ultimate truths, but as instruments to achieve their will. At its core, Chaos Magick is about the pragmatic use of whatever methods prove effective, free from dogmatic constraints. It is in this fluidity and adaptability that we discern its fractal nature—the chaotic yet patterned adaptability that enables it to resonate with the infinite permutations of human experience and desire.

Fractals in Contemporary Magickal Practice

Chaotes frequently employ sigils, symbols imbued with intention, whose creation and activation mirror the recursive processes found in fractal geometry. The construction of a sigil often involves the distillation of a desire or intent into an abstract design, a process reminiscent of the iterative steps that generate a fractal pattern. By distilling complexity into a singular form, chaotes encapsulate the essence of their will, much like how a simple iterative equation harbors the potential for infinite complexity in a fractal.

Another practice that showcases the fractal nature of Chaos Magick is the concept of "gnosis," a state of altered consciousness that chaotes enter to imbue their practices with power. This can be achieved through various methods such as meditation, chanting, or even sensory overload. The non-linear and often recursive path to achieving gnosis, with its peaks and troughs of consciousness, echoes the unpredictable yet patterned paths found in chaotic systems.

The Fractal Web of Influences

Chaos Magick does not exist in isolation; its emergence is a confluence of diverse influences forming a complex web, much like the interconnected nodes in a fractal pattern. It draws from the ceremonial magick of Aleister Crowley, the cut-up literary techniques of William S. Burroughs, and even the cybernetic theories of thinkers like Norbert Wiener. This eclectic synthesis is a hallmark of Chaos Magick, reflecting a fractal-like self-similarity where each influence contains within it echoes of the others.

The cybernetic influence, in particular, introduces a feedback loop mechanism into Chaos Magick practices. The idea that the magician's will is sent out into the universe and returns with results aligns with the feedback loops observed in fractal processes in nature, where output is fed back into the system as input, creating complex patterns over time.

The Future of Fractal Magick

As we move further into the 21st century, the principles of Chaos Magick continue to evolve and adapt, intersecting with digital technology and online culture. Cyber-magick, a new frontier for practitioners, merges traditional esoteric practices with the digital landscape, creating a fusion that mirrors the fractal complexity of our interconnected world. In the realms of virtual reality and artificial intelligence, chaotes find new canvases for their magickal workings, exploring the fractal boundaries between the physical and the digital, the real and the simulated.

In conclusion, Chaos Magick serves as a compelling contemporary manifestation of fractal mysticism. Its foundational principles—embracing change, eschewing dogma, and harnessing the power of belief—are inherently resonant with the nature of fractals, those enigmatic patterns that epitomize the harmony between chaos and order. As practitioners continue to explore and expand the boundaries of Chaos Magick, they engage in an ever-evolving dance with the fractal essence of reality, discovering new ways to manifest their will in a universe that is both chaotic and patterned, mystical and mundane.

CHAPTER 45: EXOTIC MATTER AND ANTI-MATTER: BEYOND PHYSICAL REALITY

The exploration of fractal mysticism propels us into realms that defy the common understanding of reality, casting light on substances that stretch the imagination. Exotic matter and antimatter, entities that seem to originate from the realms of science fiction, possess properties that not only challenge our current scientific paradigms but also offer tantalizing hints at deeper mystical truths.

Exotic Matter: A Gateway to Mystical Realms

Exotic matter, in the context of theoretical physics, refers to substances that exhibit properties that are completely alien to conventional matter. Most notably, it is hypothesized to possess negative mass and, consequently, negative gravity. The idea of negative gravity—a force that repels rather than attracts—seems to violate the very essence of our gravitational experience on Earth. Yet, in the labyrinthine folds of the universe, these theoretical forms of matter might not only exist but could be integral to phenomena such as wormholes, which are posited as shortcuts through space and time.

In the mystic's eye, the concept of exotic matter extends beyond its physical implications. It represents the unmanifest potential, the 'prima materia' of alchemical traditions—the raw, undifferentiated substance that is the source of all creation. Just as fractals demonstrate how complex patterns emerge from simple rules, exotic matter could be perceived as the formless seed from which the structured complexity of the universe springs forth. Its hypothesized negative mass echoes the Taoist concept of 'wu wei,' or non-action, the idea that the true nature of things is a kind of passive, effortless flow that paradoxically gives rise to all action and form.

Antimatter: The Mirror of Reality

Antimatter, the counterpart to the matter that makes up our known universe, exists as a kind of mirror image, where all the charges are reversed. When matter and antimatter meet, they annihilate each other in a burst of energy. This concept has captured the imaginations not just of scientists but of mystics as well, who see in this annihilative interaction a metaphor for the union of opposites that is central to many spiritual traditions.

The meeting of matter and antimatter can be likened to the mystical concept of the 'coniunctio oppositorum'—the union of opposites—found in Hermetic and alchemical traditions. It's the merging of the masculine and feminine, the light and the dark, the physical and the spiritual. In this alchemical wedding, the duality of existence is transcended, leading to a state of oneness, akin to the burst of pure energy released when matter and antimatter collide.

Beyond Physical Reality

Both exotic matter and antimatter take us beyond the boundaries of known physical reality, into territories that are ripe with mystical significance. They symbolize the threshold between the seen and the unseen, the known and the unknowable. If fractal patterns are the sacred geometry of the visible universe, then exotic matter and antimatter could be seen as the sacred geometry of the unseen—the mysterious, formless forces that dance at the edges of our comprehension.

In the narrative of fractal mysticism, these enigmatic forms of matter serve as a reminder that the universe is not only more complex but also more mysterious than we can possibly imagine. They stand as guardians at the gates of the unknown, inviting us to ponder the unfathomable depths of existence. Like the Mandelbrot set, which reveals ever more intricate patterns the closer one looks, the study of exotic matter and antimatter pulls us deeper into the cosmic fractal, towards an understanding that is not just scientific, but also profoundly spiritual.

The exploration of these bizarre forms of matter illuminates the interplay between chaos and order, the seen and the unseen, the physical and the metaphysical. In their peculiar properties, we find echoes of the mystical principles that have been whispered through the ages—a reminder that the fabric of reality, woven from the threads of the material and the spiritual, is a tapestry of unfathomable complexity and transcendent beauty.

In delving into the mysteries of exotic matter and antimatter, this chapter has journeyed beyond the tangible universe, brushing against the veil that separates our physical existence from the vast, uncharted territories of the mystical realm. It beckons us to contemplate the boundless possibilities that lie beyond the frontiers of current knowledge, inviting us into a dance with the divine geometry that underpins all of creation.

CHAPTER 46: TRANSCENDING LANGUAGE: SYMBOLS, SIGILS, AND SCRIPTS

In the labyrinthine corridors of human consciousness, where ideas flourish and wither in equal measure, the means of expression have long transcended the mere verbal. Chapter 46 delves into the arcane realm where symbols, sigils, and scripts serve not just as mere vessels of communication but as profound metaphysical tools that encapsulate the complexities of spiritual truths. The intricate relationship between these enigmatic symbols and fractal mysticism is a tapestry woven with threads of ancient wisdom and modern understanding, presenting a rich narrative that challenges the conventional confines of language.

Symbols: Portals to Higher Understanding

Symbols have always been a conduit for the ineffable, offering glimpses into realms that words fail to capture. Their power lies in their ability to convey vast concepts and emotions succinctly, embedding within their lines, curves, and intersections, layers of meaning that unfurl upon contemplation. In the context of fractal mysticism, symbols are the distilled essence of universal truths, acting as keys to unlock higher levels of consciousness.

Take, for instance, the ouroboros, an ancient symbol depicting a serpent devouring its tail. On a superficial level, it signifies cyclicality and the eternal return, but as one dives deeper, it unravels fractal properties — an infinite loop that is self-sustaining and self-contained. The ouroboros is not just a symbol; it's a fractal representation of the universe, where the macrocosm reflects the microcosm, a concept that echoes through the corridors of mystic traditions.

Sigils: Crafting Personal Universes

Sigils, in contrast, are personalized symbols, often created through a process of abstraction and intention. They are the architects of reality, constructed by the adept to manifest specific desires or understandings. In the tapestry of fractal mysticism, sigils are akin to unique geometric patterns, each a self-contained universe with its own laws and structures.

The creation of a sigil is a mystical process, often involving the distillation of a desire or intent into a visual form. This act mirrors the process of fractal generation, where simple rules give rise to complex and often unpredictable patterns. Sigils, once charged with the creator's will and released into the universe, function like seeds from which reality unfolds in fractal complexity, their ultimate shapes and effects often unknowable at the outset.

Scripts: Encoding the Divine

Scripts, or sacred writings, represent another dimension where language and spirituality entwine. From the elegant curves of Arabic calligraphy to the geometric precision of ancient runes, each script is an embodiment of the divine, a fractal pattern that conveys deeper wisdom. In fractal mysticism, scripts are not just collections of characters; they are maps of consciousness, each letter a coordinate, each word a path through the multidimensional landscape of the spirit.

Consider the Hebrew Kabbalah, where the letters are not mere sounds but vessels of cosmic energy. The act of writing, reading, or meditating upon these letters is a fractal process, where the microcosmic act of inscription mirrors the macrocosmic act of creation. The language is alive, dynamic, and ever-unfolding, much like the fractals that endlessly iterate across the fabric of the universe.

In conclusion, Chapter 46 unravels the intricate relationship between symbols, sigils, and scripts, and their role in fractal mysticism. These are not mere tools of communication but keys to unlock the mysteries of the cosmos, bridges between the known and the unknowable. They remind us that language, in its highest form, is not bound by syntax or grammar but is a living, breathing entity that dances to the rhythm of the universe. Through symbols, sigils, and scripts, we not only express but also shape reality, weaving our personal narratives into the grand fractal tapestry of existence.

CHAPTER 47: CONFRONTING THE ABYSS: THE ULTIMATE FRACTAL

In the penultimate chapter of our exploration into the mysterious interconnections between fractal geometry and mysticism, we delve into one of the most profound and unsettling concepts encountered in spiritual traditions: the Abyss. The Abyss, in various mystical systems, represents an ultimate void, a chasm of infinite depth, often considered to be the source or the end point of all creation. It is the esoteric heart of darkness and light, embodying both the primal chaos and the supreme order. Through the lens of fractal mysticism, we shall endeavor to unravel the enigmatic nature of the Abyss and its relation to the intricate tapestry of the universe.

The Philosophical Abyss

The notion of the Abyss permeates several mystical traditions and philosophical discourses, often representing the uncharted, the unknowable, and the ineffable. In Kabbalistic mysticism, the Abyss is the void between the sefirot of Binah and Chesed on the Tree of Life, a daunting expanse that the soul must traverse. Gnostic texts speak of the Pleroma, an abyssal fullness from which emanations of the divine emerge and return. In philosophy, the Abyss is a metaphor for existential despair, the nihilistic depths explored by thinkers like Nietzsche and Kierkegaard.

Fractal geometry provides a novel perspective on the Abyss. Just as the fractal extends infinitely in its self-similar complexity, the Abyss can be conceptualized as an ultimate fractal — boundless, unfathomable, and replete with endless iterations of creation and destruction.

Fractals, Chaos, and the Emergence of Order

At the heart of fractal mysticism lies the dynamic interplay between chaos and order. Chaos theory, which we have explored in earlier chapters, posits that within the apparent randomness of chaotic systems, there lies an underlying order, a pattern that emerges at different scales. The Abyss, viewed through this prism, can be seen as the primordial chaos, the unformed and the undefined, which paradoxically contains within it the seeds of cosmic order.

Fractal geometry demonstrates that complex and beautiful patterns can arise from simple iterative processes. Applying this principle to the concept of the Abyss, it becomes conceivable that the universe, in all its elaborate structure, could have unfolded from an abyssal singularity, a point of infinite density and potential that birthed space, time, and matter — a cosmic fractal unfolding ad infinitum.

Mystical Contemplation and the Encounter with the Abyss

Mystical practices across cultures often involve a confrontation with the void, a descent into darkness that precedes enlightenment. In the dark night of the soul, the mystic experiences an existential emptiness, a stripping away of identity and form. This spiritual abyss is not a nihilistic surrender but a passage through the fractal complexity of the self, leading to a rebirth and a profound understanding of the unity underlying diversity.

The meditative gaze into the Mandelbrot Set, a visual representation of a mathematical abyss of sorts, can be seen as a modern contemplative practice. As one zooms into the set, new patterns emerge ad infinitum, a digital abyss that mirrors the infinite depth of the soul's journey. The Mandelbrot Set becomes a fractal mandala, guiding the seeker through layers of complexity towards the ultimate simplicity of being.

The Abyss in Art and Symbolism

Artistic representations of the Abyss often utilize fractal elements to convey the complexity and profundity of this concept. Escher's infinitely descending staircases, the recursive patterns in Islamic tile work, and the intricate layers in Tibetan thangkas all capture the fractal essence of the Abyss — its endlessness and its depth. In literature, the Abyss appears as a recurring motif, a symbol of the unknown, the place where heroes are tested, and from which they emerge transformed.

The artistic exploration of the Abyss reflects humanity's perennial quest to make sense of the inscrutable, to find pattern and meaning in the void. Through art, the fractal nature of the Abyss is rendered accessible, a visual and symbolic language that speaks of the interplay between the microcosm and the macrocosm, the finite and the infinite.

The Abyss and the Future of Fractal Mysticism

As we stand on the precipice of the Abyss, peering into its depths, we are also looking forward into the future of fractal mysticism. The advances in technology and science, the evolving understanding of the cosmos, and the deepening of spiritual practices all contribute to an expanding vision of what the Abyss represents and how it can be understood.

Quantum physics, with its probabilities and uncertainties, provides new metaphors for the Abyss, while virtual realities offer simulated abysses for us to explore and learn from. The future of fractal mysticism lies in the synthesis of these diverse strands, in the continuous quest to decipher the sacred patterns that weave through the fabric of existence, from the cosmic expanse to the depths of the human soul.

As we approach the conclusion of our journey in the next chapter, we carry with us the profound insights gleaned from confronting the ultimate fractal — the Abyss. In its unfathomable depths, we find reflections of the entire universe, a cosmic echo chamber where chaos and order dance in eternal interplay, and where the seeker finds both annihilation and renewal.

CHAPTER 48: CONCLUDING REFLECTIONS: THE BEAUTY OF COMPLEXITY

As we culminate our odyssey through the labyrinthine realms of fractal mysticism, let us pause for a moment and marvel at the magnificent tapestry we've woven from the threads of chaos and order, the arcane and the empirical. The journey we embarked upon across the preceding chapters has been nothing short of a celestial dance between the tangible and the ethereal, the finite and the infinite.

Embracing the Enigma

In the embryonic stages of our exploration, we acquainted ourselves with the foundational elements of fractals and sacred geometry, recognizing these intricate patterns as the skeletal framework upon which the universe elaborates its boundless complexities. With childlike curiosity, we traced the elegant spirals of galaxies and the recursive loops of river deltas, discerning the mystical symphony that plays across all scales of existence.

As we ventured deeper into the intermediate realms, our minds expanded in tandem with the concepts we encountered. The Golden Ratio and the Fibonacci Sequence unveiled themselves not merely as mathematical curiosities, but as the underlying score to the music of the cosmos. Time, in its fractal essence, revealed the eternal recurrence of patterns, inviting us to contemplate our place within the cyclical ebb and flow of existence.

Ascent into the Arcane

Our ascent into the advanced echelons of our subject matter was marked by an elevation in both complexity and profundity. Quantum computing, multiverse theories, and Gödel's Incompleteness Theorems challenged our preconceptions and stretched the canvas of our understanding to its very seams. We peered into the abyss, that ultimate fractal, and confronted the mysteries that lay in its unfathomable depths.

Through this scholarly pilgrimage, we've encountered paradoxes and enigmas that resist tidy encapsulation. The fractal nature of our universe seems to mock our craving for linear simplicity, instead celebrating the resplendent beauty inherent in complexity. It has been an expedition that transcended mere academic intrigue, leading us into a space where science and spirituality converge, where the rigid dichotomies of matter and mind, the physical and the metaphysical, begin to dissolve.

The Awe of Interconnectedness

In this final chapter, as we weave the concluding threads of our narrative, it is pertinent to reflect on the sense of awe and interconnectedness that fractal mysticism inspires. The patterns we've studied are not isolated artifacts; they are the sinews that bind the macrocosm to the microcosm, the celestial to the terrestrial. From the spirals of galaxies to the vortices of seashells, from the neural networks of our brains to the digital realms of artificial intelligence, the fractal motif recurs with unceasing regularity, a testament to the unified fabric of reality.

This interconnectedness extends beyond the mere physical. It touches the core of our spiritual and ethical existence, urging us to consider our actions and their reverberations across the fractal web of life. It is a reminder that in the grand scheme of the cosmos, we are both insignificant and supremely important —insignificant in our fleeting physical presence, yet important in our capacity to comprehend, appreciate, and influence the cosmic dance of patterns.

The Luminous Path Ahead

As we stand on the precipice of the future, gazing into the horizon where science and mysticism continue to converge and coalesce, we do so with a sense of optimism and wonder. The journey of understanding is unending, the fractal unfolds ad infinitum, and each layer reveals new mysteries and insights. Fractal mysticism, in its union of the concrete and the abstract, the known and the unknowable, offers us a luminous path—a path that leads to a deeper appreciation of the universe and our place within its enigmatic embrace.

The beauty of complexity is not merely an aesthetic appreciation of patterns and forms; it is a holistic understanding of our existence within an intricately interwoven cosmos. It is a recognition that magic is not an ephemeral concept confined to the pages of ancient texts but a tangible reality encoded in the very structure of the universe.

In this concluding reflection, let us carry forward the sense of wonder, the hunger for knowledge, and the reverence for the cosmic tapestry that fractal mysticism has unveiled. May the sacred patterns of the universe continue to inspire, mystify, and guide us as we journey forth into the uncharted realms of knowledge and spiritual fulfillment. The dance of chaos and order, of geometry and magic, is far from over—it is an eternal waltz, and we are all participants in its grand performance.

THE END

Printed in Dunstable, United Kingdom